柔

術

Jiu

Jitsu

Complete

by KIYOSE NAKAE

Assisted by CHARLES YEAGER

The Citadel Press   Secaucus, N. J.

Second paperbound printing
First paperbound printing, 1975
Copyright © 1958 by Kiyose Nakae and Charles Yeager
All rights reserved
Published by Citadel Press
A division of Lyle Stuart, Inc.
120 Enterprise Ave., Secaucus, N.J. 07094
In Canada: George J. McLeod Limited
73 Bathurst St., Toronto 2B, Ontario
Manufactured in the United States of America
Designed by John Putnam
ISBN 0-8065-0418-8

I have known and admired Professor Kiyose Nakae for many years. He is considered the foremost instructor of authentic Jiu Jitsu in the western world. His students come from all over the world to New York City. To receive private lessons from him you have to put yourself on a waiting list and his schedule is so crowded that you may have to wait a year or two for your first lesson.

Professor Nakae has spent most of his life teaching Jiu Jitsu to Americans. When he first arrived in this country some fifty years ago he was hired to teach his skills to police departments in all parts of the land.

Professor Nakae knows thousands of tricks. From his boyhood he was drilled in the methods of the old masters of the Jiu Jitsu art. In nearly fifty years of teaching, he has boiled his system down to a compact group of tricks which comprise a complete method of self-defense and which are the easiest and most practical to learn. The dubious tricks that don't work—and which are found in so many of the books that have appeared on the subject—are *not* in these pages. The tricks in these pages work: each and every one. This alone makes it a unique product!

It is one thing to teach Jiu Jitsu in private lessons. It is quite another to teach it with a book. Only because of Nakae's deep understanding of his science and his unequalled teaching ability has such a book become possible.

Books on the self-defense arts are usually illustrated with cartoons or photographs. Professor Nakae and Charles Yeager examined these and concluded they were of little value when it came to practical learning.

A new method of showing the tricks had to be devised. Hundreds of photographs were taken of two men in action. A skilled artist then made line drawings from the photographs. I believe the result has more than justified the time, effort and expense that was invested to make such a perfect visual presentation.

My feelings were confirmed when the manuscript of this book was submitted to B. Vedel of Chicago who is probably *the* authority on books about Jiu Jitsu and Judo.

"The line drawings are a brilliant idea!" was the comment. "This is the best thing I have ever seen on the subject, and as you know, I regard books on the subject with a very jaundiced eye. This one is almost as good as actually working in class!"

There has never been a book like this one. And perhaps there has never been a time when this book was so badly needed. For in this changing world, the streets of our cities often seem like paths in a dense jungle fraught with peril.

A working knowledge of Jiu Jitsu offers the average man (or woman) an ability to cope with and triumph over a physical attacker —and to do so with ease. This, whether the opponent is larger, more powerful, or armed with knife or gun.

Mastering Jiu Jitsu has the pleasant byproduct of giving one a feeling of security in situations once packed with tensions and fears. Interestingly enough, a study has shown that a person trained in Jiu Jitsu is less likely to run into "trouble" than an untrained person. This could be because of the air of self-confidence the Jiu Jitsu-trained person possesses. Or it may be because he is less willing to become embroiled in physical violence because he knows that when he goes into action, the other guy is going to be badly hurt. Theodore Roosevelt said to "Speak softly and carry a big stick." The Jiu Jitsu student may also speak softly because he knows that his skill is a very big and very damaging stick.

The book you hold in your hands is not a plaything. Jiu Jitsu is serious business and must be studied and practiced until the student is skilled in the art.

I was tempted to say "in the almost lost art" for a lost art it has almost become. Jiu Jitsu is no longer taught in Japan. It is no longer passed from generation to generation, as it had been for hundreds of years. And here I should explain that Jiu Jitsu is not Judo—and the two should not be confused.

Judo is a sport and a worthy one. Its popularity is very much on the increase, and many believe the time will soon come when Judo is an Olympics sport.

There is a surface similarity about some of the movements in Judo and Jiu Jitsu—but there the likeness ends. Judo, of course, derived much from Jiu Jitsu.

However Jiu Jitsu is an art of self-defense which was developed with skill and precision as the exclusive property of Japanese nobility.

Judo is played for points. Jiu Jitsu is played "for keeps." With Jiu Jitsu you may, as you desire, punish, damage, or even kill your opponent.

With Jiu Jitsu, David may defeat Goliath. Thus the beauty of the art is that it relies for success not upon brute strength but upon finesse and the ability to win by seeming to yield.

One last note before you enter the portals of your Jiu Jitsu classroom. As the publisher, it was my original plan to price this book at $6. Though the volume is small, its production costs were large and would justify the $6 price. But then it was decided, for sentimental reasons, to price the book at $5. For $5 is the cost of a single forty-five minute lesson with Professor Nakae. And here is the course for the price of a single lesson!

Lyle Stuart

To
the generations of men before us
whose lifetime devotion to the
art of Jiu Jitsu has made this
book possible.

FOREWORD

Jiu Jitsu is a method of defense and offense without weapons in personal encounter. For many centuries in Japan it was practiced as a military art, together with fencing. archery and the use of the spear.

Jiu Jitsu is not a contest of muscular strength. Nor is its prime purpose to maim or kill, but merely to incapacitate one's opponent for the time being by means of simple tricks and holds.

Jiu Jitsu tricks and holds are very simple. A thorough knowledge of them, gained only with constant practice, should develop in one a feeling of strong self-confidence. This confidence causes the Jiu Jitsu expert to react almost instinctively in the event of a sudden attack and to maneuver any situation to his own advantage.

Professor K. Nakae is one of the few living masters of authentic Jiu Jitsu. As Chief Instructor of New York's Dojo (Judo academy) I have seen many books written on this subject. This book is unusually good for the simple and clear illustrations and captions are readily understood by the beginner. And they derive from genuine knowledge and skill.

George G. Yoshida

1. The Beginning

You are about to take an intelligent and progressive step which should provide mental and physical benefits for you not only in the immediate future but for the rest of your life. You are about to begin training in Jiu Jitsu.

Jiu Jitsu tends to wipe out the differences of size, weight, height and reach. The possessor of the skill gains tremendous self-confidence and the ability to walk without fear.

Skill and knowledge are in themselves sufficient to subdue any aggressor no matter how strong or vicious. You are always ready for action, unarmed, in any situation, regardless of the direction from which the attack comes.

The first lesson you must learn is poise and assurance. You learn to be mentally cool and alert in the face of danger, and you begin to experience a self-restraint which comes only with supreme self-confidence.

Jiu Jitsu Complete was written to fill the definite need at this time for a more practical, a more complete and more authoritative course on the subject than has heretofore appeared.

Jiu Jitsu is a word which consists of two parts: *jiu* means "gentle, pliable, virtuous, to submit" and *jitsu* means "art or science." In meaning and in fact, Jiu Jitsu depends not on brute strength but on psychology, knowledge of anatomy, and skill that comes from practice in making certain movements with your body.

Practice—and lots of it—is essential. To become an expert in the complete art requires years of training. However a few simple tricks which may be adapted to any emergency are enough to put mastery in the hands of the average person who must defend himself against an assailant who has superior strength or who may be armed.

Jiu Jitsu is not Judo. The tricks in this book are dangerous and must be practiced with extreme care. In Judo, a modified derivation from Jiu Jitsu, friends can compete because real danger-tricks have been removed and because certain rules and prohibitions are imposed in order to avoid injury to the participants.

Not so with Jiu Jitsu. Jiu Jitsu is dangerous business and should be used only in case of emergency where "anything goes" for the sake of self-protection.

Strength is not a major factor in Jiu Jitsu. Rather, balance, leverage and speed are needed, for then available strength is applied to its greatest advantage.

Women can become proficient in Jiu Jitsu. In many tricks, the stature of a woman, the softness of her arms and the sharpness of her heels are exceedingly potent weapons. Moreover, women need Jiu Jitsu. Many a girl owes her life to a slight acquaintance with its tricks.

As sex is no barrier to learning, so age is no barrier. Newspapers recently told of a 72-year-old frail man who, with Jiu Jitsu, disarmed a youthful robber who was forty pounds heavier than he. The old man held him with ease until the police arrived.

Even the police often have a need for Jiu Jitsu. In my lifetime I have demonstrated and proven the superiority of this science to police departments in Yonkers, Chicago, Philadelphia, Pittsburgh, Detroit, Memphis, Syracuse, Toledo, Montreal and Indianapolis.

Many police officers have enrolled with me for private lessons.

I hope you will never be in a position where your life is endangered. But if it is, I am confident that what follows will prove of value to you—if you learn it.

Good things take time. Do not hurry through this book. Practice each trick diligently until you know it well.

As you learn new tricks, keep practicing the old ones. This review and practice is important. Especially since I am going to give you the most difficult tricks first. Only practice, practice and more practice will give you proficiency in Jiu Jitsu.

Let us begin then by acquainting you with a classification of Jiu Jitsu's tricks.

There are the exercises and the break-falls.

There are throws and holds and combination tricks. There are breaking tricks. And there are practical applications of Jiu Jitsu such as the defense against a knife or a club or a gun or a blow with a fist.

For the complete list of the tricks we are going to learn, turn the page. As you become good in the application of a trick, check it off. You will be pleased to discover how quickly they come to you once you have mastered the first few.

Now, with a minimum of further talk, we shall get to the exercises.

You will find that the instructions which accompany each illustration are brief and to the point. Read them carefully. No words have been wasted—and every word is meaningful if you are to progress as you should.

Although a gym (wrestling) mat is not essential—it is quite helpful. If the use of one is not available to you, a thick rug or any surface softer than cement or hard earth would be helpful for learning and practicing. In place of carpeted floors, a soft lawn or a sandy beach is suitable.

When practicing the tricks which follow, dress in old clothes or shorts. Your clothing should be loose enough to permit free comfortable movement.

CLASSIFICATION OF TRICKS

4. BREAKING TRICKS

How to free yourself from strangle and other holds

5. PRACTICAL APPLICATION

Practical means of avoiding blows from any direction
and of throwing, and holding.

Practical means of protecting yourself against an
opponent armed with a knife, and of disarming,
throwing or holding.

Practical means of protecting yourself against an
opponent armed with a club, and of disarming,
throwing or holding.

Practical means of protecting yourself against an
opponent armed with a pistol (and within reach),
and of disarming, throwing or holding.

6. ARTS FOR EMERGENCIES

The lessons in this course are not furnished you in
exactly this order since it is frequently more in-
teresting for the student to learn as he progresses
how throws may be combined with blows, etc. However when you have learned all the lessons in this
book, you may wish to practice them in this order as
a logical system.

EXERCISES

PURPOSE: To train the muscles to extend and contract freely, and the joints to function smoothly in every part of the body.

A

B

A.—Lift arms, extend forward and pull back in loose flowing motion, the fingers opening and closing alternately. Do this 6 times. Then extend the arms over the head and back to the shoulder in the same manner for 6 times.

B.—Extend arms forward, move them in large circles, the right arm clockwise, the left counter clockwise Do this 6 times then reverse.

C

D

C.—Place your left palm on your left hip, with fingers pointing to the floor. Push body forward and to the side, straighten up and repeat with right hand. Alternate 6 times.

D.—Stand on left foot and move your right foot in the air in circles. This exercises the hip joint. Lift the right heel to the buttock and down again, this exercises the knee and ankle joints. Repeat with the left. This is good practice for balancing on one foot, which, as you shall see, is important.

E

E.—Half raise arms and lean back, then lean forward, bending knees, and touch the floor with your hands.

NOTES.—Remember, these exercises are for flexibility and not for strength. They must be done slowly, with body held loosely. The muscles and joints must never be tightened.

FALLS.—The right way to fall must be learned in the beginning for you will take many falls in learning Jiu Jitsu. Once you learn to do this easily and safely you will not fear falling and this will make your movements free, rapid and uninhibited. This enables you to concentrate on the offense instead of thinking only of the defense.

See Next Page

Break Fall No. 1

FALLING BACKWARD SITTING POSTURE

A

Raise both arms, cross at the wrist and bring to shoulder height. (1)

B

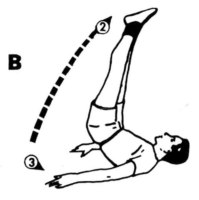

Roll backward, raise both feet together (2). Hit mat with both hands (3).

CONTINUED ON NEXT PAGE ▶

NOTE:—As you roll back, pull your chin to your chest and watch your belt. This protects your head from hitting the mat or ground. Falling back should be like rolling a wheel, the feet raising automatically. The hands hit when shoulder blades touch the mat. Fingers held straight together (lightly), hitting with the whole arm. This BREAKS the fall. Kick up with both legs at moment of hitting. This stops you from rolling over.

Break Fall No. 2

FALLING FORWARD

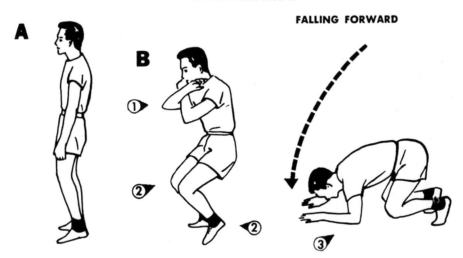

A

B

Raise arms as in "B" (1). Raise heels and bend legs (2).

Kneel on mat, continue forward motion of body and land on arms from fingertips to elbows (3) arms extended in direction of body.

Break Fall No. 3

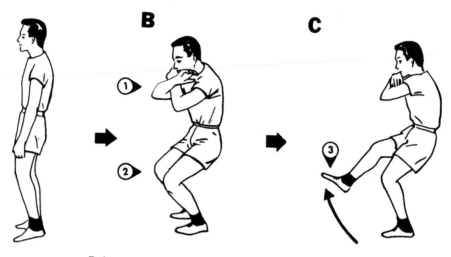

A   **B**   **C**

Raise your arms as in "B" (1). Bend legs at the knees (2).

Raise one leg (3).

Break Fall No. 4

FORWARD SOMERSAULT

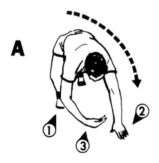

A

Step forward a little outside with right foot (1) bent forward, place left hand on ground palm down (2) ahead of left foot. Put right hand on ground palm up (3) between left hand and left foot.

B

Push your body forward, throw up left leg, turn body over as in "B."

BREAKFALL No. 4. (C) After practicing a while you will find that there are different ways of finishing.

    (1) One leg in the air
    (2) Both legs in the air
    (3) Halfway getting up
    (4) Getting Up

C

Finish as in "C."

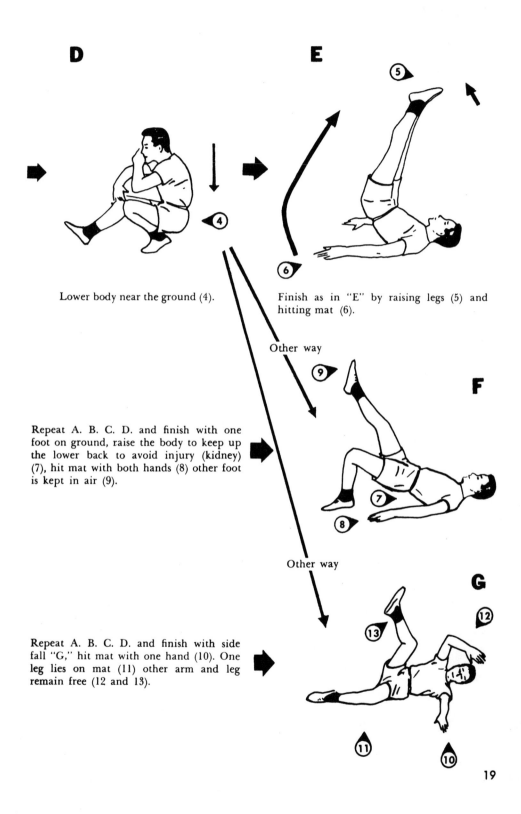

D

E

Lower body near the ground (4).

Finish as in "E" by raising legs (5) and hitting mat (6).

Other way

F

Repeat A. B. C. D. and finish with one foot on ground, raise the body to keep up the lower back to avoid injury (kidney) (7), hit mat with both hands (8) other foot is kept in air (9).

Other way

G

Repeat A. B. C. D. and finish with side fall "G," hit mat with one hand (10). One leg lies on mat (11) other arm and leg remain free (12 and 13).

19

Breaking–Opponent Strangles from Front

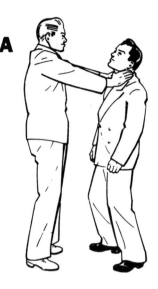

A

If opponent attempts to strangle with two hands from side . . .

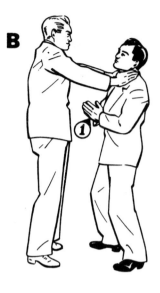

B

Put your hands together (1).

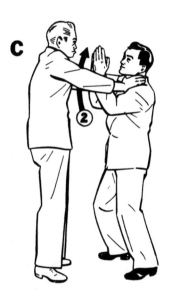

C

Swing your hands up between opponent's arms (2).

D

The impact of your arms against the inside of his arms will break the hold.

In this situation, opponent's weak spot is his elbow. The idea is to apply pressure with your arms against his elbows. Now try the next trick, which is just as easy.

Breaking–Opponent Strangles from Front

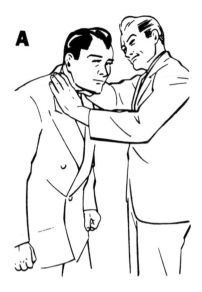

If opponent attempts to strangle you with one hand back of your neck, one hand in front of neck, and his head in close; or both hands choking from side; or in any case in which opponent holds you with his face in close . . .

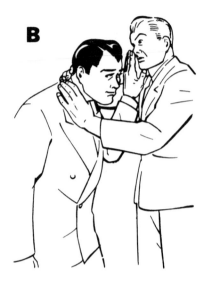

Smear his nose up and back with either hand.

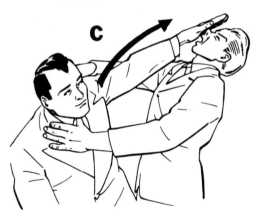

This will put you in the position shown above. Opponent will cry, temporarily blinding himself. You will be free and able to start almost any of the throws or finishing tricks to be described later.

Frequently, when an opponent attempts to choke, or in any case when he holds you from the front, a strong blow to the nose with the base of the hand is all that is needed to break the hold.

Remember that when you have finished either this or the previous trick, you have merely freed yourself. But this is not enough. You must either hold opponent in a helpless position or must apply punishment if you really mean to protect yourself.

Many different ways to hold or punish an opponent will be taught you in this course. But because there are so many tricks, you may be tempted to ask, "Why are they all needed?" No matter how good a medicine is, it is not good for every case. Therefore, it is wise to have many kinds of medicine available, so that if one does not work, another may be tried.

Likewise, there are many different parts of the body which can work together or individually. The knowledge of many tricks will enable you to protect yourself even if both hands are incapacitated—by using the feet. Or if your feet are held—by using your hands. Or you may find yourself seated when the attack comes.

When you have finished this course you will be master of many tricks, and will be able to protect yourself regardless of your position when danger comes.

Breaking-Opponent Hugs from Rear, Underneath Arms

If opponent attempts to hug you tightly from rear, underneath arms . . .

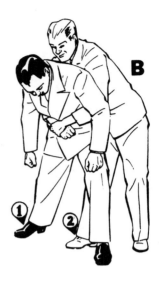

Take a long step to the right with your right foot (1) so that opponent's right knee is behind your left thigh. Bend forward and prepare to seize opponent's right leg (2). (If opponent holds very tightly, push against his stomach sharply with your hips.)

Drop hips, bend over and seize opponent's right leg with both hands (3). Now lift his right leg quickly (4) with your hands while pressing down against his right leg with the back side of your left thigh.

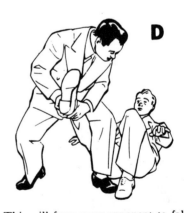

This will force your opponent to fall.

VARIATIONS

If your opponent holds you with one hand underneath your arm, and the other hand over your shoulder and mouth, you can free yourself by a blow from your elbow to his neck.

If opponent holds as shown in "A," you can also free yourself by a blow with elbow to his chin. If blow is hard enough, it will knock opponent out.

Or if opponent holds as in "A," you can also free yourself by a sharp blow with the back of your head to his chin. If opponent is too short for a blow to his chin, the same blow against his nose or forehead will be equally effective.

Or you can free yourself by a back-kick to opponent's knee with the sole of your foot.

Pencil Holding Trick

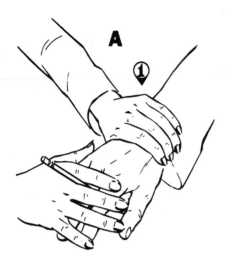

Hold a pencil or fountain pen between your second and third fingers. With your other hand (1), grasp opponent's wrist, and lift up to about waist level (2). Slide pencil between any two of his fingers.

Position of bodies at start of trick.

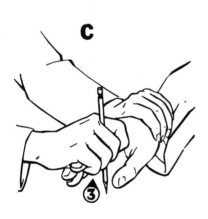

Now close your fingers around opponent's fingers, and squeeze (3).

The pencil will cause severe pain and force opponent to submit.

DO NOT FORCE

If you try a trick and it doesn't succeed, don't wilfully attempt to force the trick to work. Change to some other trick. Often this strategy gives even better results because the first attempt has caused opponent to assume an unbalanced position. At this moment almost any trick will work with great success, because you have led your opponent into a position where his strength and weight work to his disadvantage.

Assume your opponent attempts to push you. Hesitate a moment. Then step back suddenly, instead of pushing him back. He will lose his balance. At this moment try some trick suitable to his position, and you will find it easy to throw him. But remember that no matter how good a trick is, you will not be successful unless you apply it while your opponent is in the right position.

Intentionally act to excite your opponent, and watch for the moment when he is off guard. Then apply your trick, or combination of tricks. *But this action should be, mechanical, automatic—done without thinking—the result of much practice.* When you have achieved this proficiency, you can use your knowledge and ability against an opponent in any position, in any situation; against a group, or against weapons.

Do not try for too much speed at first. Practice every movement correctly step by step. After you have gained the proper understanding of the movement, you can then increase your speed. Naturally, speed is very important.

Again we remind you that it is essential that you practice all movements with *relaxed* mind and body.

NOTE FOR YOUR OPPONENT IN PRACTICE

Whenever a trick is improperly used against you, and is not effective, do not fall for the sake of appearances. Otherwise your partner will never learn. But remember, do not try to resist and do not forcibly move against the action, for you will either be hurt or you will find yourself in a still more vulnerable position. Also, you will force your opponent to call on his reserve strength which results in a serious possibility of sprain or fracture.

GIRL HAD TRICK TO OVERCOME THUG

Los Angeles, Oct. 29 (A. P.).
—Mary Bischel, attractive 20-year-old telephone operator, told the police that she was walking down the street when a man clutched her from behind.

Quickly she leaned forward, grabbed his ankle, reared back and planked him flat on the pavement. Then she stomped on his face and fled.

"I don't remember where I learned that stunt," she explained, "but maybe it was from the boys in my neighborhood."

Posture

POSTURE is important because the body must have a strong foundation to impart power to a trick.

This "A" shows a natural posture, comfortable, relaxed, well-balanced, with each foot under its corresponding shoulder. This is the best position for both defense and offense. Your hands are inside his arms resting lightly above his elbows, and all your muscles and joints are relaxed and ready for any move. This is a most convenient posture from which to move in any direction.

It is essential to be relaxed because this permits free, quick movement. Moreover, relaxation permits the use of full power at the point of attack since there is no waste of power at some other point.
You may practice any trick, starting with this posture.

Balance

An ordinary chair serves to demonstrate the importance of breaking balance in Jiu Jitsu. The chair, solidly resting "flat on its feet," is strong; difficult to overthrow. If you push it, it is likely to slide rather than fall over.

Tilt the chair so that it rests on only half its normal base. Now it requires much less energy to make it fall.

C

Tilt the chair even further so that you take away still more of its balance. Now it requires very little energy to make it fall.

Balance

Suppose you face, instead of a chair, an opponent who is 50% heavier and stronger than you are. By matching your strength against his strength, you will obviously never overthrow him. His position is strong, like that of the chair in "A."

But suppose he attempts to push you. If instead of resisting, you yield by retreating a little faster than he is advancing (at the same time retaining a hold on him), he will be forced to lean forward in an unbalanced position, similar to that of the chair in "B." Because of his awkward position, he will have momentarily lost two-thirds of his resisting strength, and your strength (if you have kept your own balance) is now approximately twice as great as his.

If, at this point, you also break his balance to the side, as with the chair in "C," he will have lost so much of his resisting power that it will require very little strength to make him fall to the ground.

* * *

If your opponent is standing erect, and is not resisting, it is easy to break his balance to the right or left, forward or backward, by a light pull or push, or by lifting or pressing. If opponent is resisting, you can break his balance just as easily by pushing or pulling in the direction in which he is resisting, thereby using some of his strength to accomplish your purpose.

The foundation principle of Jiu Jitsu is balance and relaxation. This must be learned first.

When relaxed, it is easier to maintain balance, act quickly, change position suddenly. And you can bring power to the spot where it is needed without wasting any of it. You need all your power, so waste none of it.

Sweeping Calf No. 1

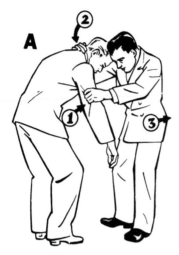

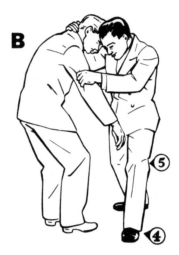

With your left hand, grasp your opponent's right arm behind his elbow (1). Place your right hand behind his neck. Pull down (2). Push your hip back and bend chest forward (3).

Keep pulling down on his neck and step forward with left foot to a point 10 or 12 inches outside of your opponent's right toes. Left toes point a little to outside (4). Keep balance on your left leg, and bend left knee (5). Bend chest forward for balance and power. Your head almost rests on opponent's right shoulder. Keep both feet on ground; do not release your hold on his neck. Hold this position momentarily.

Now try the following case

Breaking – Opponent Holds from Front

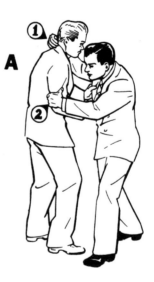

If opponent holds your coat collar or shirt front with one hand or both hands, and pulls, or bends his elbow . . .

Place your right hand back of his neck and pull (1), and at same time grasp his elbow with your left hand (2). Step forward with your left foot in preparation for Sweeping Calf No. 1.

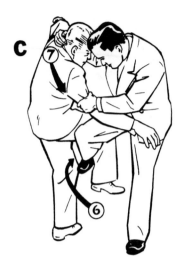

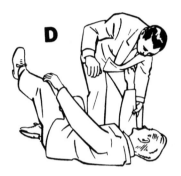

Now quickly sweep your right upper calf *up* against opponent's right leg or to side of the knee-joint (6). At same time your right arm presses opponent's shoulder to the direction of your left foot (7). As you sweep with your calf, bring your foot around in a circling motion and lift your heel up high. Use only leg strength (from knee-joint down). When opponent starts to fall, release your right-hand hold. However, keep your grip on his right arm to hold him afterwards and (in practice) to keep opponent from falling too hard.

Opponent will fall.

Now you can throw opponent with Sweeping Calf No. 1. Remember that after you step forward with your left foot, there is a momentary pause before sweeping back with your right foot; the purpose of this is to gain better balance and more power for the sweep-back.

You can also break this hold by a sharp blow to the nose with the heel of your hand.

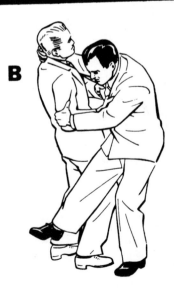

Sweeping Calf No. 2 with Shoulder Scissor

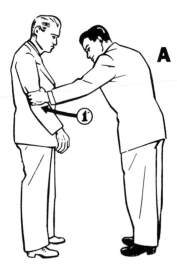

A

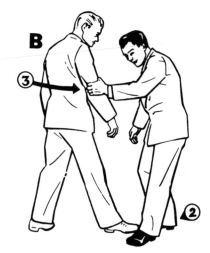

B

With your left hand, grasp your opponent's right arm just in back of elbow (1).

Step back a little with your right foot (2). Pull his elbow toward your right (3), using only hand power. Bend forward a little. This puts your opponent in half-turned position.

Alternative (calf sweeping), from "C" wrap your right leg around his right leg from the outside, holding contact with your thigh, calf and heel. Tighten your leg grip raising his leg with yours, hold his leg

tightly in your knee joint, to prevent his releasing his leg. Pull his captured leg behind you with your leg, bending your left knee slightly and bring him down *with leg power alone.*

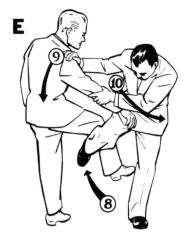

E

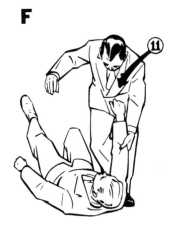

F

elbow as shown (10). As you sweep with your calf, bring your foot around in a circling motion and lift your heel up high. Keep your hip steady. Keep chest bent. Use only your leg strength (from knee-joint down).

Opponent will fall heavily on his back. If you are standing too far away after he falls, step in closer, to be ready for the next movement. Keep body bent forward (11).

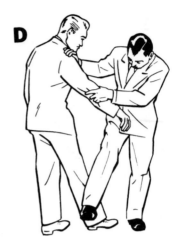

Turn your body and both feet to left (4). Place your right hand or arm on top of opponent's right shoulder *or* left shoulder (5). Shift your balance to left leg, and bend left knee (6). Keep chest forward (7). At this point be sure you are relaxed; otherwise you cannot finish. Hold this position momentarily (as you would just before striking a golf ball, to be sure your balance is set).

Now quickly sweep your right upper calf *up* against opponent's right leg behind or to side of the knee-joint (B). Your right hand or arm presses opponent's shoulder around to the direction of your left foot (9), and your left hand pulls opponent's

Tip for beginners: Picture "E." Sweeping up opponent leg first (8). Press his shoulder next (9) then pull his arm until his fall (10). Use your power against one point at a time. This means your power will con-

centrate in one point. Practice any other tricks the same way until you learn well. After much practice all these movements will come simultaneously.

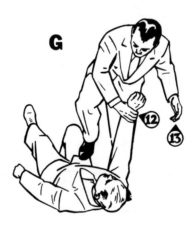

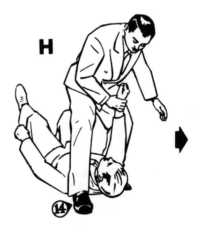

Gently grasp his right wrist with your right hand (12), using the hold shown; and free your left hand (13). Or you can hold with

both hands. Place your right foot over his left shoulder (14).

Bend your left knee (15).

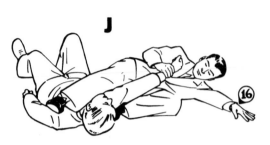

Fall naturally, straight to your left side. Support balance with your left hand, palm down (16). Retain your hold on his hand.

This is a double lock—simultaneous arm lock and strangle hold (shoulder scissor). It is an almost perfect hold, from which escape is practically impossible. Use pressure against neck only when necessary; continuous pressure will cause unconsciousness. Be careful in practice. If opponent taps twice on your body or the ground, this is signal he has had enough. In this throw, and all other throws, several finishing tricks can be used. Likewise, most finishing tricks can be used with a wide variety of throws. To save your time, and to avoid confusion, most of the finishing tricks have been grouped for separate study in a subsequent session.

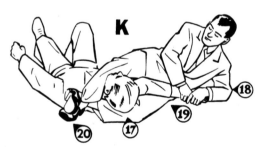

Extend your left leg under his neck and right shoulder (17). Rise up on your left elbow (18), and bring opponent's elbow against left leg with his palm up (19), and lock your feet as shown (20). Now press his arm down while squeezing his neck with your legs. Both hands must hold opponent's wrist above the wrist joint; or you can hold your right wrist with your left. Right knee joint must be against opponent's neck.

A Reminder

Are you having difficulty learning the tricks? Does it seem to you that you will never learn correct balance?

Do not become discouraged. You are taking private lessons and so you cannot see the other pupils are having the same difficulties. Nor should you forget that the experts were once just as awkward as you are now—maybe more so!

It takes time to overcome the tense habits of a lifetime. It takes time and much effort to learn to relax your body. Jiu Jitsu balance, however, is so natural that your progress will be rapid.

In another few weeks you may wonder how you ever could have been so stiff and so clumsy. So remember again: the other fellow, the one who performs Jiu Jitsu so well, was once as rigid and as worried as you are now.

Cheer up, Beginner!

"Spooning" Ankle Throw No. 1

A

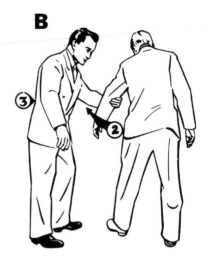

B

Stop just far enough away to be able to grasp opponent's arm firmly. With your left hand, grasp his left arm just behind elbow (1).

Pull opponent's elbow toward your left (2), using for the most part hand power. Keep your balance on your left foot. Bend your left knee, and incline upper part of your body forward (3).

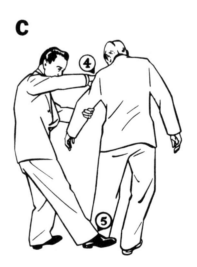

C

Place your right hand on opponent's left shoulder from behind (4). Place the instep of your right foot against opponent's left ankle (5). Point your right toes in a little, pigeon-toe fashion.

Reminder: Your action should be against one point at a time. Picture D (6) first (7) next then (8) for finishing. Also may be used following the next tricks: Spooning Ankle Throws No. 2 and No. 3.

In any trick where you are on one leg and ready to use the other leg, you must help your balance by holding him with a good grip of your hand or hands. Remember, power comes from a strong foundation.

柔
術

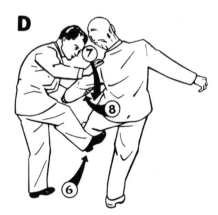

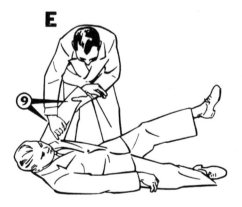

"Spoon" your right foot against opponent's left ankle from behind in direction of his toes (6). Not necessary to put all your strength in this. Your right hand pulls opponent's shoulder toward your right and presses downward (7); and your left hand pulls his elbow toward you (8).

Opponent will fall on his back. Keep your grip on opponent's arm after he is down; this will help in the holding trick you use to keep him down (9).

"Spooning" Ankle Throw No. 2

A

This shows "Spooning" Ankle Throw when you grasp opponent's *right* arm instead of left (1). Pull opponent's elbow to your right (2), using principally hand power.

B

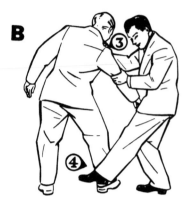

Place your right hand on his right shoulder, from front (3). Place the instep of your left foot against opponent's right ankle (4).

C

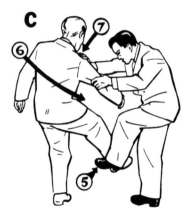

Point your right toes in a little, pigeon-toe fashion. "Spoon" your left foot against opponent's right ankle from behind in direction of his toes (5). At same time your left hand pulls opponent's elbow toward your right (6), and your right hand presses downward toward your left (7).

D

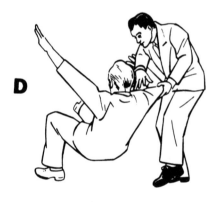

Opponent will fall.

This trick illustrates the analogy between Jiu Jitsu and fishing. When you drop the hook in the water, it swings free and the string is relaxed. When the fish bites, you pull suddenly, a quick moment of power and you catch him. If the fish then runs you give him more line. When he relaxes you pull in. In the case above, the moment of quick power comes when you "spoon" with your foot and pull down with hand.

"Spooning" Ankle Throw No. 3

A

B

C

Step forward on your left foot (1) and make your right foot free (2). Push back opponent's upper arm very lightly with your left hand (3) to make him hold his weight on his right foot (4).

Place the instep of your right foot against opponent's left ankle from behind (5) and spoon your right foot against opponent's left ankle from behind in direction of his toes (6). Then your right hand pulls opponent's upper arm downward (7).

D

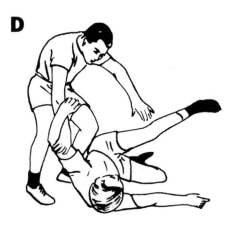

COMBINATION TRICKS: Illustrations below show how to work out combinations of tricks. Obviously all possible combinations cannot be illustrated. You can make up many more. Drawings below are taken directly from tricks referred to, and should not be taken too literally when practicing.

Their purpose is merely to *suggest* the action. You are supposed to *know* the tricks before trying to apply them in combination. *In fact, you cannot understand these instructions unless you have already practiced the tricks referred to.*

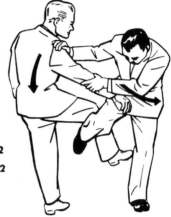

SPOONING ANKLE NO. 2
TO SWEEPING CALF NO. 2

If opponent resists, or if you miss for any reason at this point in applying Spooning Ankle No. 2 (Session 1) . . .
You can transfer your weight to left foot and go into Sweeping Calf No. 2 (Session 1). This shows the advantage of using leg power from knee down in applying Spooning Ankle No. 2; otherwise it would be difficult to shift from the one trick to the other.

BREAKING—OPPONENT STRANGLES FROM FRONT TO SWEEPING CALF NO. 1

After you break opponent's strangle hold as shown (See Breaking—Opponent Strangles from Front, Session 1) . . .

You can go into Sweeping Calf No. 1

PENCIL HOLDING TRICK— TO SPOONING ANKLE NO. 1

From position "D" in Pencil Holding Trick (Session 1) . . .
You can go into Spooning Ankle No. 1 (Session 1). In this case change the position of your left hand from his wrist to his shoulder, catch his arm with your right hand and spoon with your left foot. (A good point to remember in "spooning" is to put all the power possible into your big toe.)

SWEEPING CALF NO. 1— TO SPOONING ANKLE NO. 1

 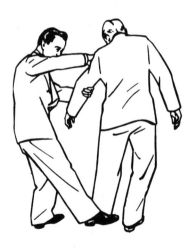

If you start to throw opponent with Sweeping Calf No. 1 (Session 1), and opponent steps back with his right foot instead of coming to the position shown at left . . .

You can go into Spooning Ankle No. 1 (Session 1) without even changing the position of your hands. But in this case, when he steps back, take a step straight forward with your left foot, before spooning with your right foot, and you will have stronger balance and greater power.

39

Session 2.

This session contains the following lessons:

Spring Hip Throw,
Breaking—When Opponent Strangles from
Front,
Over-Shoulder Throw,
The Knee Whirl,
Defense Against Blow with Fist,
Breaking—When Opponent Strangles from
Rear,
Breaking—When Opponent Strangles from
Rear,

and a bonus trick—
Breaking—When Opponent Holds Wrists.

Before you start on this session, we again want to emphasize the value of serious, consistent practice—the importance of learning each trick so well you can do it without thinking. Do a thorough job on each trick before going to the next. Only through practice can you gain the self-confidence you need. Review Session 1 today. Please go back and read the page on Balance and Relaxation in Session 1. This is all-important. Jiu Jitsu, which means gentle or soft art, naturally indicates a relaxed mind, and body. Of course, the principle of relaxation, and the technique of breaking balance, cannot be learned overnight. But there is no reason to feel discouraged if they seem to come hard at first. It merely takes time and patience. The point is to keep them always in mind when you practice this course.

Spring Hip Throw

With your left hand, grasp opponent's right arm just behind elbow (1). Step with your left foot to a point inside opponent's left foot (2). Push back your hips, and incline your chest forward (3).

Now, shift your weight to your left leg (4).

Bend your knees (7) so that your hips go low as shown. Push hips back against opponent to strengthen your balance. While you are turning into this position, your right arm should encircle opponent's waist and pull his chest and abdomen in as close as possible against your back. Now your hips can support his entire weight.

Quickly spring your hips up. And swing forward with your right shoulder (8) as if you were throwing a sack of potatoes over your right shoulder.

C

Turn, spinning on the ball of your left foot (5).

D

Go completely around, so that your hips are full against opponent, and a little to the right of him (6-next picture).

G

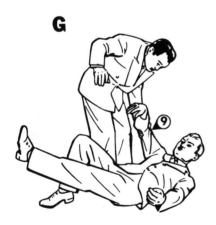

Opponent will fall on his back. Keep your hold on his elbow or arm (9). In practice, keep your right hand around opponent's waist and hold him up as much as possible to keep him from falling too hard.

Breaking–Opponent Strangles from Front

If opponent attempts to strangle from front as shown. . . .

Step in with your left foot to the front of your right foot (1). Strike the inside of his right elbow with your left forearm, forcing it aside; and place your left hand on his right arm (2).

This shows how action is continued with Spring Hip Throw.

Strike the inside of his left elbow UP-WARD with your right forearm (3). This brings you into position for any Hip Throw, or Over-Shoulder Throw· (next trick). NOTE: When breaking, do not push opponent back, or you will not be able to apply Hip Throw. This is why his right arm is pushed UPWARD.

Opponent falling in Spring Hip Throw.

The Knee Whirl

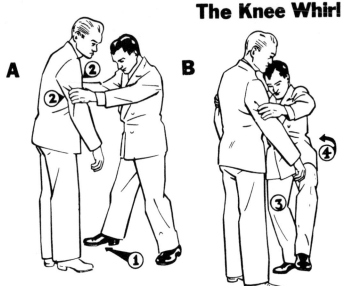  

A **B** **C**

Stand, or step in to a point just far enough from opponent so that your hands COULD rest firmly on his arms. Now, step forward with your right foot to a point outside his left foot (1). At same time grasp his arms (2).

Shift weight to your right leg. Bend your knee (3). Drop hips slightly and twist them to your right (4).

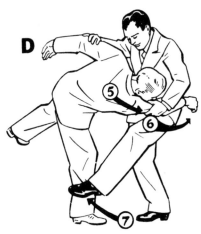

D

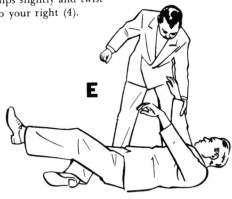

E

Your left hand now pulls in a wide outside circle (5). Your right hand merely follows through, pushing in the direction opponent is falling (6). At same time swing your shoulder and hip to right. Now quickly stop his knee (7) by placing the sole of your left foot against opponent's right leg just below and to the outside of his knee. Keep pulling. Follow through.

This action will cause opponent to fall.

NOTE: Your left instep against opponent's right leg keeps him from moving to recover his balance. Do not kick him in this action, but merely place your foot FIRM-LY against his leg. Important: The inside of your left calf must face almost straight up. In practice, occasionally try this trick without using your right hand, to gain a clear idea of the principles of balance involved.

Also practice trick against opponent's left knee, reversing all foregoing instructions. If opponent stands with one leg back (either leg), you will get better results by applying your foot against knee which is back.

Over-Shoulder Throw

A

With your left hand, grasp opponent's right arm just behind elbow (1). Step with your left foot to a point inside opponent's left foot (2).

B

Now, shift your weight to your left leg, and turn (3) . . .

C

Spinning on the ball of your left foot (4), go completely around, so that your hips are full against opponent and a little to the right of him (see next picture).

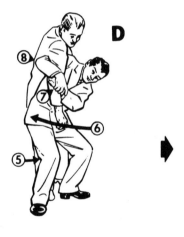

D

Bend your knees (5) so that your hips go low. Push hips back against opponent to strengthen your balance (6). While you are turning into this position, slip your right hand under and around opponent's right arm, grasping your own left wrist (7). Your back should be close against opponent's chest and abdomen, and your right upper arm (not shoulder) underneath opponent's right armpit (8).

CONTINUED ON NEXT PAGE

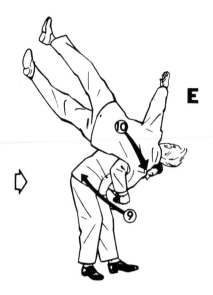

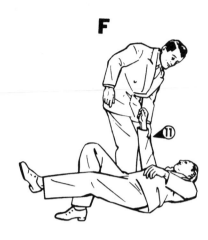

Now, quickly spring your hips up and back (9). At the same time, incline your body forward and pull opponent's shoulder downward with both hands (10). Opponent will go over your shoulder as shown.

This trick is the same as the Spring Hip Throw except that instead of encircling opponent's back with your right arm, you slip your right arm under and around opponent's right arm, and pull DOWN-

Opponent will fall on his back. Keep your hold on his elbow (11). In practice, hold opponent up as much as possible by means of your grasp on his arm, to keep him from falling too hard.

WARD with both hands. This trick is not recommended when there is a considerable difference in your height and that of opponent. It is most effective against a person of approximately your height.

Pull opponent back a little and GRADU-ALLY squeeze his neck on all sides, squeezing with your arms and pushing with your head and shoulder. The push of the head is more important than the pull of the arms.

This trick must be practiced with care. It is likely to make your opponent unconscious before he is aware that he is going. It is not a punishing hold but a real strangle, cutting off the breath and applying pressure against carotid arteries. Strangle holds are ideal for women since they do not require a hard, strong arm. As a matter of fact, a woman has a real advantage. The softness of her arms means that more of the flesh will be in contact with opponent's neck, applying pressure more evenly (thus more effectively) all around.

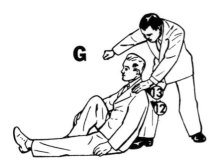

To finish, pull opponent up to position shown. Place your right knee against his back (12). Place your left hand LIGHTLY on his shoulder (13), without pressing. In this manner you can keep him from getting away. But do not press heavily on his shoulder for this will allow him to escape.

Rest your left knee on ground about 18 inches back of opponent (14). Place your right arm over opponent's shoulder and around his neck (15) so that your forearm is against front of opponent's neck, and so that the back of his head rests against the muscle in the center of your upper arm. With your left hand (on top of shoulder as shown), grasp your right wrist (16). Place the side of your head against opponent's head just back of his ear.

For another strangle finish when opponent is seated, get in a position back of opponent with your left knee up (17) and your right knee on the ground. Place your right arm over his right shoulder and around his neck as shown. Bend your right hand back over opponent's left shoulder (18). With your right hand, grasp your left arm (19) (which should already be extended over opponent's left shoulder) a little above elbow (with your right palm down). Pull opponent back a little. Place the palm of your left hand against back of opponent's head as shown. Now you can strangle by pulling with your right arm while pushing with your left. You will thus apply pressure against his throat in front and against the carotid artery on the right side of neck.

REGARDING USE OF STRANGLE HOLDS

There are two types of strangle holds:
1) Using coat collar. 2) Using arms or legs around the neck.

This course shows only a few principles involved in holds of the second classification. These holds are more practical and may be used in any emergency.

Neck holds can be used alone or in combination with other tricks. They involve pressing or squeezing against the throat or carotid artery. The result is to stop breathing or the blood supply to the head. This makes opponent dizzy or unconscious, puts an end to his resisting power, and makes him temporarily *hors de combat*.

However, whenever it is necessary to use a neck hold, be exceedingly careful. THE MAN WHO HAS BEEN RENDERED UNCONSCIOUS BY A NECK HOLD WILL NOT REVIVE AUTOMATICALLY. HE MUST BE BROUGHT BACK BY EXPERT RESUSCITATION.

Neck holds are usually applied when opponent starts to rise after the throw. It is most important to act quickly before opponent can fully recover himself.

There are several positions in which opponent might fall as the result of a throw, hence the various neck holds shown in the course start from various positions.

Neck holds are so simple that women, and even children, can use them easily against more powerful opponents.

Defense Against Blow With Fist

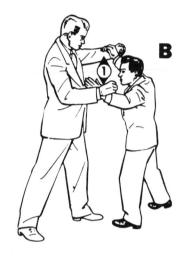

If you face an opponent from whom you expect trouble, perhaps a blow with the fist . . .

Move in closer to opponent with either foot and block opponent's intended action by throwing both hands inside and against opponent's arms as shown (1), or to front of opponent's shoulder, blocking his arms with your elbows. The idea is to tie up his arms so that for the moment he cannot strike. Use just enough strength to stop his action, but do not push him. If he steps back, repeat the action to keep close to him.

NOTE: If opponent attempts to strike low, throw your arms DOWN to stop the action. Then use any finish described.

If opponent attempts to strike at your head, open your hands and throw them *up*, striking his arms with the back of your hands. If he attempts to strike with only one hand, use only one hand to block the action.

If opponent strikes high with one hand and low with the other, block the first action by throwing one hand high, and the second action by throwing the other hand low.

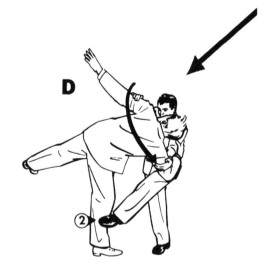

Now you can finish by The Knee Whirl (2).

C

Come in closer in preparation for throw.

E

Or by Spooning Ankle Throw (3).

F

Or by Sweeping Calf Nos. 1 or 2.

Breaking–Opponent Strangles from Rear

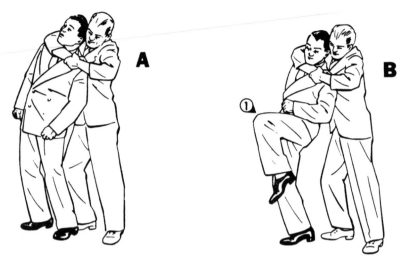

If opponent attempts to hold from rear—using strangle or other hold in which his body is fairly close to you . . .

Lift your knee high (1) and . . .

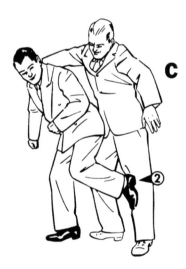

Kick back with a good solid blow to the knee-cap (2). Be careful in practice. The knee-joint is easy to break.

It is also effective, particularly for women, to kick inside of opponent's shins, or stamp on his feet with the sharp heel. Either one is a punishing blow.

Breaking–Opponent Strangles from Rear

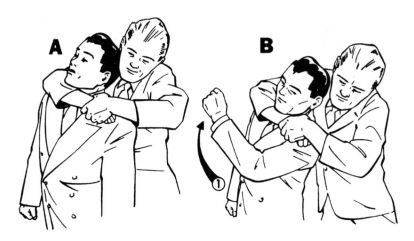

If opponent attempts to strangle from rear as shown . . .

Bring left arm forward (1).
Close fist tightly.

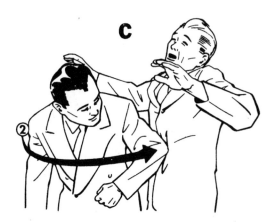

Swing your body and elbow fast — all to-gether, one motion — and strike opponent in solar plexis or stomach with elbow (2). Occasionally, opponent will hold so tightly that there is no room to swing your elbow. Then a sharp blow with the back of your head to his chin or nose will cause him to loosen his hold long enough for you to get in an elbow blow.

Or you can free self with a strong back-kick to knee.

Breaking Wrist Hold

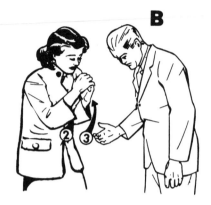

If opponent attempts to hold left wrist with right hand . . . grasp your left fist with your right as shown (1).

Keep left elbow low and close to body (2). Bring up left fist, as shown, in direction of left shoulder (3). Use the strength of left fist. Right hand merely guides left. Opponent will not be able to hold.

If opponent holds both hands as shown . . .

Another method of breaking this hold from position shown in "C":—Instead of pulling up as in "B," press DOWN with the arm which is on top (using only forearm power and without moving shoulder), against opponent's arm, forcing him to release hold. At same time free your other arm by lifting it up with a quick, short motion, and you will be in an excellent position for a throwing trick.

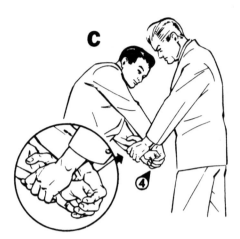

C

④

If opponent holds your left arm with two hands . . . extend your right hand between his arms, and grasp your left fist (4). Now lift up as in "B."

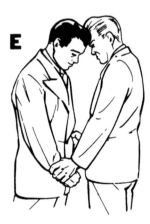

E

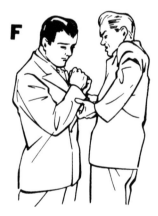

F

Step in closer. Hold elbows close to body. Lift up fists inside opponent's arms. He will not be able to hold.

For women it is sometimes easier to kick opponent's shin before breaking hold by lifting arms. The kick disconcerts opponent and lessens his resistance.

If opponent holds your arms at the elbow, or any point higher than shown, the trick is still easier.

This trick can be accomplished just as easily by a woman if she will first bring her head forward as if she intended to strike opponent's face or chest with top of her head. This disconcerts opponent, and gives more strength to the arms.

COMBINATION TRICKS: Illustrations below show how to work out combinations of tricks. Obviously all possible combinations cannot be illustrated. You can make up many more. Drawings below are taken directly from tricks referred to, and should not be taken too literally when practicing.

Their purpose is merely to *suggest* the action. You are supposed to *know* the tricks before trying to apply them in combination. *In fact, you cannot understand these instructions unless you have already practiced the tricks referred to.*

IF OPPONENT GRABS YOUR NECK WHEN YOU TRY OVER-SHOULDER THROW

If you attempt the Over-Shoulder Throw (Session 2), and opponent succeeds in getting a strangle hold on you as shown in second picture above . . .

You can break his hold and floor him by a blow with your elbow to his solar plexus as shown in Breaking—Opponent Strangles from Rear (Session 2).

If opponent holds so tight that a blow with either elbow cannot be very effective, start hitting at him with both elbows and you will loosen his hold enough to permit a good hard blow with one elbow.

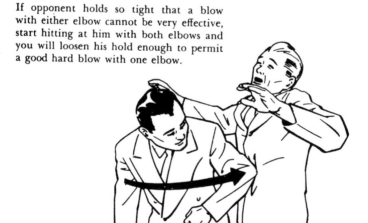

If opponent attempts to strangle you as shown (from Breaking—Opponent Strangles from Front, Session 1) . . .

You can reach up and grasp his arms and go into The Knee Whirl (Session 2). In this case it is not necessary for you to break his strangle hold with your arms. He will automatically release his hold as he starts to fall.

IF OVER-SHOULDER THROW FAILS TO WORK FOR YOU

If you get opponent to point shown here in Over-Shoulder Throw (Session 2), and for some reason cannot finish . . .

You can immediately release your hold on opponent, drop your hands and catch opponent's legs by reaching through your legs as shown in Breaking—Opponent Hugs from Rear, Underneath Arms (Session 1) and finish as described therein.

Session 3.

This chapter contains the following lessons:

Sweeping-Side Hip Throw
Breaking—When Opponent Hugs Tightly
Hand Throw No. 4—Arm Pressure Against Knee

Shoulder Lock
Elbow Lock (Down) No. 1
Bent-Arm Wrist Lock
Defense Against Blow with Fist (Four Lessons)

You will note that Hand Throw No. 4 is given in this lesson, although the first three hand throws have not yet been given. This is to enable us to present more of the popular lessons on Defense Against Fist in this session.

Regarding Combinations of One or More Tricks

By now you may be wondering what to do when you start a trick and find that for some reason you cannot finish it. At this point your knowledge of combinations—or changing from one trick to another—becomes important. By resisting your initial action, your opponent will always provide the opportunity for still another trick. Obviously, therefore, combination tricks are more difficult to resist and are consequently more effective. More combinations than you will ever need will be given to you in Session 6, after you have learned enough basic tricks to be able to make the most intelligent study of such combinations. Meanwhile, you will be able to work out many combinations of your own through practice.

Sweeping-Side Hip Throw

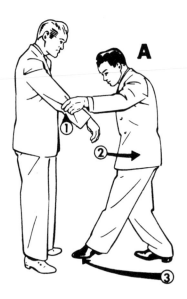

With your left hand, grasp opponent's right arm just back of elbow (1). Push your hips back (2). Step with your left foot to a point between opponent's feet as shown (3). (Note direction in which left foot is pointed—outward to left.)

Now, shift weight to your left leg; make a turn to your left (4) . . .

Now, hold tight with your left hand (9), and powerfully slide the back of your right thigh up and against the outer side of his right thigh (10). At the same time, swing your hips and shoulder to the right (11).

Opponent will fall.

Your right hip now comes in contact with, and goes a little to the right of, the lower right front of opponent's body (5). Keep your left leg bent as it supports your entire weight (6). Encircle his waist with your right hand (7). Extend your right leg to outside of opponent's right leg as shown (B). Your body leans a little to the left. Push your hips back a little. Pull opponent in as close as possible to your body, and bend forward a little. This effectively breaks his balance.

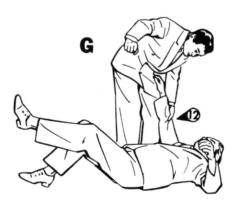

Keep your hold on his right elbow (12) in readiness for a finishing trick.

Breaking–Opponent Hugs Tightly

If opponent hugs as shown, you can break his hold by bringing your knee up sharply to crotch.

If opponent hugs VERY TIGHTLY, push both his knees (1), or just one knee, back by flexing your knees forward, as shown, keeping your weight on the balls of your feet. This will force opponent to move back which will then provide the opportunity to bring your knee up sharply to crotch.

With Jiu Jitsu, David may defeat Goliath. Thus the beauty of the art is that it relies for success not upon brute strength but upon finesse and the ability to win by seeming to yield.

After you have flexed your knees as shown in "B," you can throw opponent by circling into the Sweeping-Side Hip Throw. In this case your left hand holds opponent under his waist with your right arm (2), and going arm (3).

This shows continuation of Sweeping-Side Hip Throw.

Opponent will fall.

Hand Throw No. 4–Arm Pressure Against Knee

Face opponent.

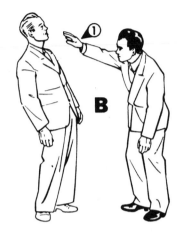

Extend your right hand, aiming fingers at opponent's face (1). Move your face and shoulders forward at same time. Do not move too fast, however, for the intent is merely to make oponent THINK you are aiming for his EYES. This will make him lean back as shown.

When you drop down to apply wrist against knee, the action should be very swift, without warning, a complete surprise to opponent. It should be done before opponent has an opportunity to make another move.

CAUTION: This trick is dangerous. There is a strong possibility of fracture or dislocation. Once pressure is applied, your opponent must fall or the knee will break. So be careful in practice. Rehearse very slowly at first.

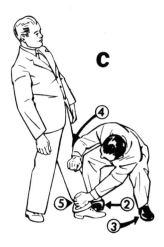

Step forward a little with your right foot (2). Simultaneously (with a little jump) step back with your left foot (3) and drop down as shown. (You can rest right knee on ground, if you wish.) Bring your right arm down so that the sharp edge of the outside of your wrist crosses opponent's leg at right angles just above the knee cap (4). (Always remember to apply trick against leg which is nearest you.) Your left hand grasps his ankle with your fingers behind ankle (5).

Now push with your right arm, using only forearm power, while holding firm with your left hand. While doing this, the front of your chest should be at right angles to the direction opponent faces.

If, in position shown above, opponent stands with knee stiffly bent forward, so that you find it difficult to apply pressure downward, quickly rise to standing position and apply Sweeping Calf Throw No. 1.

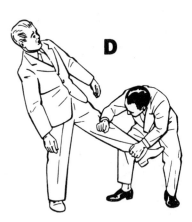

This shows how opponent will fall.

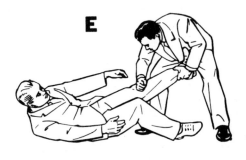

As a result of pressure against his knee, opponent will not be able to support his weight and must fall. But remember, it is the PUSH against the knee—and NOT the pull on the ankle—which throws opponent off balance.

Shoulder Lock

Extend left hand inside opponent's arm as shown (1). Extend right arm over his arm and back of his upper arm (2). Keep left fist closed for strength (3).

Step with left foot to front of opponent (4), so that your foot points to opponent's left. Bring his arm across your left shoulder (5). This is easily done by lifting your left hand. Bend your neck a little to left. Make his elbow point skyward (6).

Elbow Lock (Down) No. 1

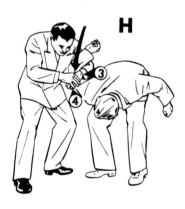

As in "A" above, extend left hand inside opponent's arm and extend right arm over his arm and back of his upper arm. Now wrap the fingers of your right hand back of opponent's arm (1), just above the elbow. Now pull with your right arm to your right to the point shown above (2). Incline your body forward to put your weight into this motion. (In beginning this trick, your arm joints must be relaxed and free.)

Continue pressing opponent down. Keep your left arm near opponent's elbow to lock his arm more securely (3). Place right hand over left wrist and hold as shown (4). Now step around so that you face at right angles to opponent. Keep opponent's arm parallel to ground. Do not press his arm too far down and you can hold him in this position indefinitely.

Press his elbow with your two arms (7). This brings opponent to this position.

Now slide your left arm to the right until your elbow comes to his arm (8), and grasp your left wrist with your right (9). Shift weight to left leg, bend left knee a little (10), and bring left shoulder forward in the direction to which your left foot points.

EXAMPLE

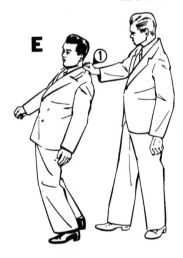

If opponent grabs your collar from behind with his right hand (1) . . .

Turn about a half turn to left. Swing your left arm around and over his right as shown, holding his wrist against your neck. (This is same idea as in Shoulder Lock.) Now hold opponent with Shoulder Lock as in "D."

Bent-Arm Wrist Lock

With your right hand, grasp opponent's right wrist gently as shown (1).

Step to his right side (2). Turn so that you face in same direction as opponent. Raise his arm as shown. Slip your left arm under his elbow (3).

REGARDING USE OF JOINT LOCKS:

Holding tricks which involve bending, twisting and stretching the joints cause great pain, stop opponent's movement and put him in a helpless position. There is an almost endless number of holding tricks, varying with opponent's position. In this course we show those which are the most useful, and the easiest to learn.

With your left hand, make opponent bend elbow as shown (4).

Now place your left hand over your right hand (5).

Press DOWN on his hand with both your hands (6). Now you can easily hold him.

NOTE: Be sure that the back of opponent's upper arm rests against the crook of your left elbow and that his elbow is close to your left side, in order to hold him tightly. Keep his hand high, near your chin, and press DOWN—NOT toward your body.

Defense Against Blow With Fist

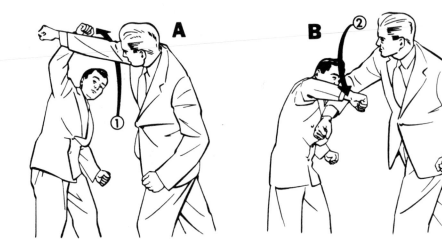

If opponent attempts to strike high with his right, move left foot to side, lean your body to left, duck head a little to left, and at same time make his blow glance off your right forearm (1).

Hook your right arm over opponent's right arm as shown (2).

A Reminder

Are you having difficulty learning the tricks? Does it seem to you that you will never learn correct balance?

Do not become discouraged. You are taking private lessons and so you cannot see the other pupils are having the same difficulties. Nor should you forget that the experts were once just as awkward as you are now—maybe more so!

It takes time to overcome the tense habits of a lifetime. It takes time and much effort to learn to relax your body. Jiu Jitsu balance, however, is so natural that your progress will be rapid.

In another few weeks you may wonder how you ever could have been so stiff and so clumsy. So remember again: the other fellow, the one who performs Jiu Jitsu so well, was once as rigid and as worried as you are now.   Cheer up, Beginner!

Step in front of opponent with your left foot (3), and place left wrist against the back of his upper arm (4).

Press against his arm with your left wrist (5), with power and movement coming from your left wrist.

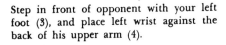

This trick must be done very quickly, in one continuous motion. In defense against blow with fist, speed is of utmost importance. Otherwise opponent will withdraw his arm before you can lock it. Therefore, practice this trick until you can do it even without thinking.

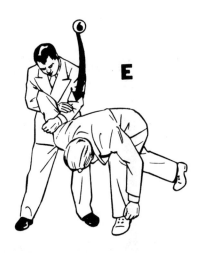

Continue pressing to position shown. Your right hand grasps your left forearm, for stronger pressure. Do not bend your waist, but drop your left shoulder to apply your weight against his arm (6).

Defense Against Blow With Fist

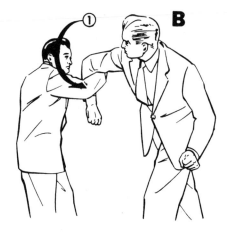

If opponent strikes high with right, block as shown.

Hook your right arm over opponent's right arm (1) and clamp his arm tightly in position shown above.

NOTE: This trick is very similar to the preceding trick. The difference is that in the preceding, opponent's arm is stiff, straight out, with his fist at your right side. In this trick, his arm is bent, with his fist between your body and his.

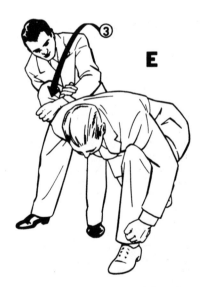

Step in front of opponent with left foot.

Place left wrist behind opponent's arm and start pressing (2).

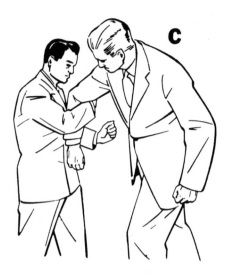

Continue pressing (3) to position shown. Your right hand grasps your left forearm, for stronger pressure. This is Elbow Lock (Down) No. 2 (not shown elsewhere).

Defense Against Blow With Fist

If opponent attempts to strike low with his right, block his blow by means of your left forearm against the inside of his forearm (1). Step in with left foot as shown (2).

Hook your left arm around opponent's arm (3) and lift his arm up until it rests on your shoulder as shown (4).

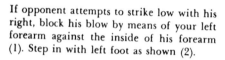

Defense Against Blow With Fist

If you face an opponent from whom you expect trouble, perhaps a blow with the fist ... move in closer to opponent with either foot and block opponent's intended action by throwing both hands inside and against opponent's arms as shown, or to front of opponent's shoulder, blocking his arms with your elbows. The idea behind this is to get in closer to opponent and clinch while tying up his arms so that for the moment he cannot strike. Use just enough strength to stop his action but do not push him. If he steps back, repeat the same action to keep close to him.

If opponent is very heavy—or tall—it is preferable to finish with Spring Hip Throw instead of Sweeping-Side Hip Throw.

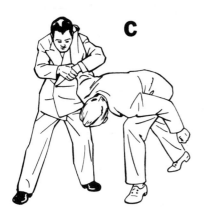

Finish with Shoulder Lock.

Now you can finish him by a Sweeping-Side Hip Throw. This time, instead of circling his waist with your right arm, capture his left arm at the shoulder with your right arm (1), holding loosely.

If you desire to throw by arm pressure against knee, throw opponent's hands up as you block him in "A."

COMBINATION TRICKS: Illustrations below show how to work out combinations of tricks. Obviously all possible combinations cannot be illustrated. You can make up many more. Drawings below are taken directly from tricks referred to, and should not be taken too literally when practicing.

Their purpose is merely to *suggest* the action. You are supposed to *know* the tricks before trying to apply them in combination. *In fact, you cannot understand these instructions unless you have already practiced the tricks referred to.*

SPRING HIP THROW— TO SWEEPING-SIDE HIP THROW

If you get opponent to position shown in Spring Hip Throw (Session 2) and find that for some reason you cannot finish . . .

You can change to Sweeping-Side Hip Throw (Session 3) and your chance of finishing will be extremely good.

BREAKING STRANGLE HOLD— TO HAND THROW NO. 4

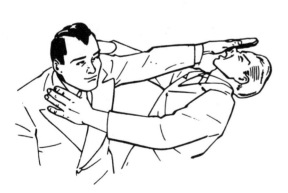

After you have broken opponent's strangle hold by smearing his nose back as shown in Breaking—Opponent Strangles from Front (Session 1) . . .

You can drop down and apply Hand Throw No. 4 (Session 3) against whichever knee is forward.

HAND THROW NO. 4—
TO SWEEPING CALF NO. 1

If you get to this position in applying Hand Throw No. 4 (Session 3) against opponent's knee, and if he resists or if for any reason you think you cannot finish . . .

If you get opponent to position shown here in Sweeping-Side Hip Throw (Session 3) and he resists . . .

Quickly arise and apply Sweeping Calf No. 1 (Session 1). NOTE: Be sure to apply Sweeping Calf against the same leg you were working against with Hand Throw No. 4.

You can add much greater power to the throw by bringing your right leg way forward and swinging it back hard against opponent's leg, at same time bringing his body around as described in this throw.

Session 4.

Session 4 contains:

You have now been given instruction in more than fifty self-defense tricks (counting throwing and finishing tricks separately). If you have been practicing diligently, you are well on your way to becoming expert in the art of self-defense.

But we emphasize again and again that there is no substitute for actual practice. Some of the tricks are so simple, fundamental and natural that you will never forget them even after a few practice sessions. But the harder tricks need more work, if you desire to vary your defense and offense in such a way as to confuse completely your adversary. Try to practice a little every day, if possible. Remember to practice slowly at first, then gradually try for speed.

There are many joint tricks in this course that are very useful in self-defense, especially against an armed attacker. Such tricks must be done quickly, so that your opponent may not realize what is coming and avoid it or pull away. If your trick is done swiftly you will succeed, but the necessary speed may injure or even break the captured joint. This is especially true if he resists and you increase the force at that point. Therefore you must remember to practice such tricks with extreme care.

Elbow Lock (Up)

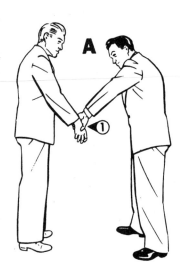

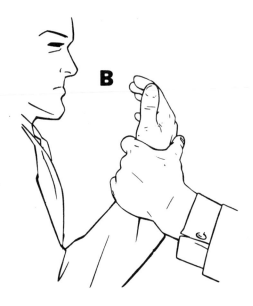

With your left hand, grasp opponent's right hand (remember, same side of body) as shown (1), so that your thumb is on the back of his hand and pointing down, and your fingers are inside his palm.

Turn his hand counter-clockwise and bring up to this position (about face height).

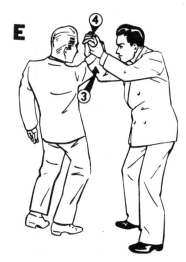

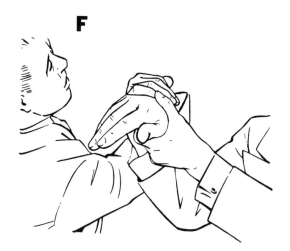

Push up with your right arm until opponent's elbow is about his face height (3) and his forearm is almost parallel with the ground; then place the fingers of your right hand on top of opponent's wrist as shown (4).

This shows position of hands in "E."

C

D

Now bend your right arm and slip it back of opponent's elbow (2).

This shows position of hands and arms in "C."

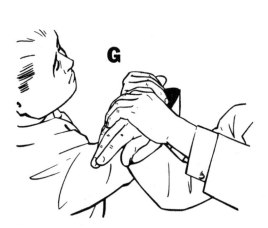

G

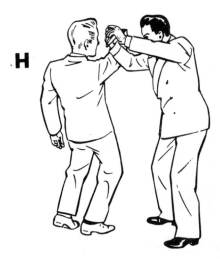

H

Now shift your left hand to a position on top of his right hand as shown, and grasp his hand firmly, with your thumb going underneath his hand.

NOTE: Remember, do not pull opponent toward you. But hold him away from you by keeping your arm stretched out. This keeps him off balance and prevents him from using his left hand against you.

Step back a little with your left foot so that you face in opposite direction from opponent. Shift your weight to left leg. Now bend both knees slightly for better balance and push UP with your right elbow. This will hold him.

Straight-Arm Wrist Lock

A

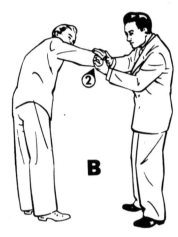

B

With your right hand, grasp opponent's right wrist as shown (1), so that your thumb is on the back of his hand.

Raise opponent's arm to position shown. At the same time, grasp his hand with your left hand (2). Now clamp both hands tightly around opponent's hand so that he cannot jerk it away.

Note in "B" the position of opponent's hand and arm. His palm is facing outward and not quite straight up. His arm is turned outward so that the little finger points up. The elbow points upward at an angle. THIS IS IMPORTANT. If his arm is turned farther, he will be able to turn his back to you. However, if this happens, you can avoid danger from his free elbow by holding it with your left hand.

You can also prevent him from turning his back to you by applying extra pressure with your right hand.

When in position shown in "C," you can free your right hand and strike his elbow with the side of your right hand. This will dislocate elbow; use only in emergency.

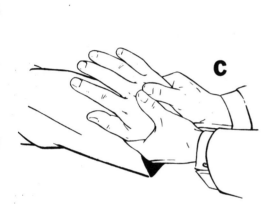

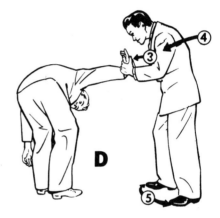

This shows position of hands in "B."

While opponent's arm is in position shown in previous picture, your thumbs start pressing his hand back toward his elbow (3). Bend your chest (4). While pressing, use only your hand strength. This pressure will cause him to go down. Step back a half-step with both feet (5). Spread feet apart a little for better balance, greater strength, and freedom of movement. Now bend your knees and drop hips a little, and continue to press just enough to keep him in position shown. (More pressure will cause him to go to his knees, which is not desirable.) Keep a 90-degree angle between his arm and body which prevents the possibility of his kicking at you.

If he takes a step forward, do likewise to preserve the 90-degree angle. If he goes to his knees, simply drop your hips lower and you can continue to hold him.

A Reminder

Are you having difficulty learning the tricks? Does it seem to you that you will never learn correct balance?

Do not become discouraged. You are taking private lessons and so you cannot see the other pupils are having the same difficulties. Nor should you forget that the experts were once just as awkward as you are now—maybe more so!

It takes time to overcome the tense habits of a lifetime. It takes time and much effort to learn to relax your body. Jiu Jitsu balance, however, is so natural that your progress will be rapid.

In another few weeks you may wonder how you ever could have been so stiff and so clumsy. So remember again: the other fellow, the one who performs Jiu Jitsu so well, was once as rigid and as worried as you are now.　　　Cheer up, Beginner!

Finger Holding Trick

With your left hand, grasp the two outside fingers of opponent's right hand (1).

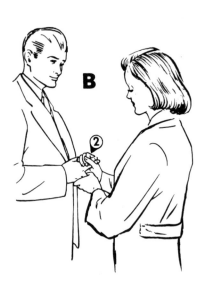

With your right hand, grasp opponent's other two fingers as shown (2).

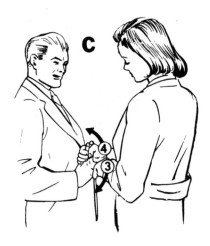

Now bend the two outside fingers down (3) while splitting the other two fingers back (4). You will cause him to go down in a helpless position.

A variation of the foregoing: With your right hand, grasp the two outside fingers of opponent's left hand (5).

With your left hand, grasp opponent's thumb as shown (6). Your left thumb should point toward opponent.

Now split his thumb back while splitting his two fingers down. This will cause him to go down and you can easily hold him.

Strangle Hold No. 1 from Rear

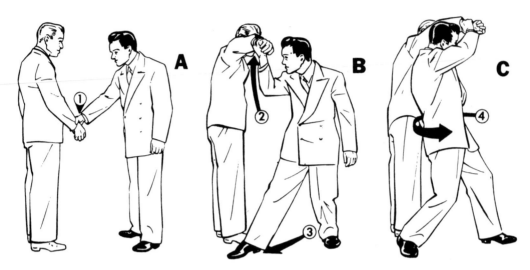

With your right hand, grasp opponent's right wrist (1).

Lift opponent's arm as high as your head (2), and take a long step with your right foot to his right side (3).

Turn your body (4) so that your face in same direction as opponent.

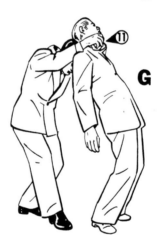

Move your head to back of opponent's neck (9). Push your hips back for better balance (10). Press with your left hand and your head, and at same time pull opponent back off balance and hold him there. This makes him stand on his heels. But do not pull him too much or he will fall; and do not stand too close at this point, to guard against his free elbows and feet.

Now free your right hand and with it grasp the fingers of your left hand (11). You thus have opponent in a helpless position in which you can punish him severely. The purpose of this hold is to subdue a dangerous opponent, not to injure him. Press just hard enough to accomplish aim.

Note in this picture that hands are applying pressure against bottom of chin, not against the throat. And wrists press against back of opponent's shoulders which prevents him from turning or using his arms.

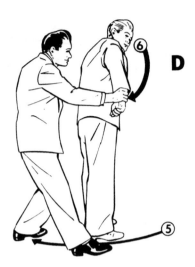 **D**

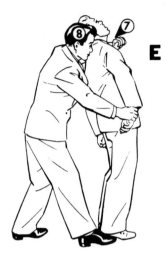 **E**

Place your left foot about 18 inches back of opponent's left foot (5) and bring his right hand down a little (6).

Bring your left arm OVER opponent's left shoulder and around his neck so that the back of your hand is against his throat, just under chin (7). Place the top of your head against back of opponent's ear (8) to stop his movement temporarily.

In practice, to signal your partner to release a strangle hold, tap twice on some part of his body or slap twice on the mat or ground.

Remember that while the foregoing trick has been explained step by step, the action is really continuous without a stop. The whole trick should require about one second.

Illustrations "A," "B," "C," "D" merely show the best way to get behind your opponent from a facing position at start. This phase of the trick is, of course, unnecessary if you happen to start from rear of opponent.

It is necessary to hold opponent's right hand until your left arm is around his neck, as in "F." Up to this point his right might be dangerous. However, after your right

hand has grasped your left wrist, he cannot use his elbows or feet against you. But keep both arms over his shoulders to prevent his using either hand effectively.

In case opponent attempts to protect his neck by lowering his chin, press his nose upward with your left wrist. This will give you an opportunity to drop your left arm down against his neck. Or, if you prefer, keep pressing his nose.

If opponent happens to be standing with back to wall (this will also work in any case), grasp his wrist tightly. Then spin quickly to your left, going underneath your own arm. Keep a tight grip on his arm. This will force opponent around to position shown in "D." Then proceed as directed in "E," "F," and "G."

Defense Against Blow With Fist

A

If opponent attempts to strike with right fist . . . move left foot to side (1), incline your body to left, duck head a little to left, and at same time make his blow glance off your right forearm (2).

B

Grasp his right wrist (3) and step forward with right foot as shown (4).

C

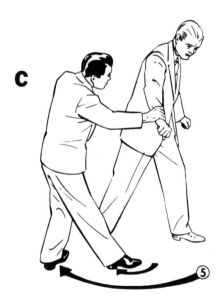

Now place left foot behind opponent (5), spinning on the ball of your right foot into this position, and prepare to get strangle hold.

D

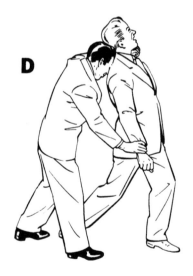

Get Strangle Hold No. 1.
From position "C" you can finish with almost any of the arm locks shown in this course. Or from position in "C" you can throw opponent with Spooning Ankle Throw No. 1. Or "C" is a good position for a kidney punch with your fist.

柔術

Strangle Hold No. 2 – from Front

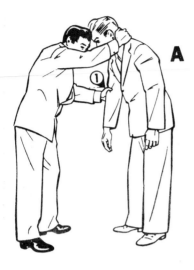

A

Face opponent.
Grasp opponent's right arm with your left hand (1). Place your right hand back of opponent's neck. Pull forward as shown.

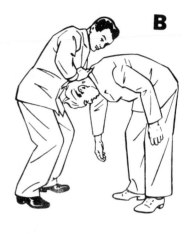

B

Keep pulling his head down toward your stomach.

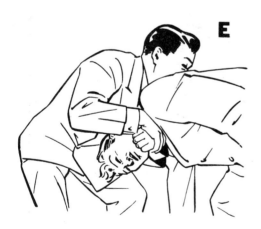

E

Without pulling him forward, step back a little and spread your feet slightly. This makes your position still stronger.

Or

Arms all the way around his neck.

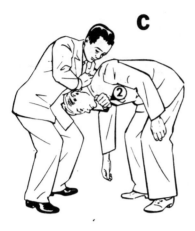

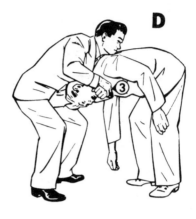

Place your left forearm under opponent's chin, against his neck (2), and keep the back of his head against your stomach. Bring your left arm around very quickly to block any possibility of his reaching you with his hands. But don't squeeze his neck at this point.

Place your right arm likewise under opponent's chin, and grasp your left wrist with your right hand (3). Keep your back, neck and head as stiff as a board. Press your chin against his spine, and your stomach and chest against his head. Hold steady. Do not push down. Press against his throat with both arms.

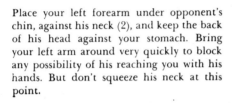

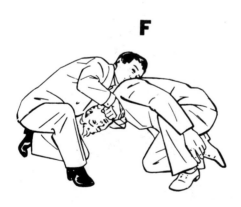

If opponent attempts to drop to his knees, follow him down as shown.

In "D," "E," and "F," if opponent tries to reach you with his arms, you can stop his arms by bringing your elbows forward.

For another, still stronger, strangle hold, (starting from position in "B") wrap one arm around opponent's neck as far as it will go. Bring your other arm around and place it over first arm. Then squeeze all around with your arm and chest.

Also you can hold opponent's head on either side of your body (about waist height) with the same finish.

Breaking — Half-Nelson

A

If opponent attempts to hold with Half-Nelson as shown . . .

B

Bend forward. Push against his front with the back of your hips. Using your strong neck muscles, bring your head up sharply (direction is against his wrist) while pressing his arm forward with strong shoulder power. Put all the power you can into this.

E

This shows position in "D" viewed from front. Place your left arm in front of his abdomen (2). Bend knees and drop hips a little. Keep your body bent forward, and your chest down.

F

Lift his right leg from behind with your left knee (3), and at same time push back with your left forearm. This will cause opponent to fall. Or, you can give him a sharp blow to the solar plexus (or the chin) with your elbow for a knockout.

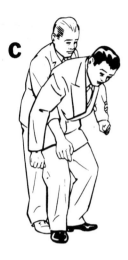

C

Opponent will be unable to hold.

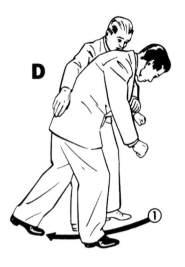

D

Place your left foot behind opponent to his right leg (1).

Note: If opponent still holds after you have followed instructions in "B," push his right knee back with the sole of your right foot. This will free you.

Or, if opponent holds very tightly in position "B," clamping your shoulders, you can clamp his arm with yours, and drop hips straight down (maintaining good balance). Now get opponent on your back and throw him with Spring Hip Throw.

Breaking- Full-Nelson

A

If opponent attempts to hold with Full Nelson...

A Reminder

Are you having difficulty learning the tricks? Does it seem to you that you will never learn correct balance?

Do not become discouraged. You are taking private lessons and so you cannot see the other pupils are having the same difficulties. Nor should you forget that the experts were once just as awkward as you are now—maybe more so!

It takes time to overcome the tense habits of a lifetime. It takes time and much effort to learn to relax your body. Jiu Jitsu balance, however, is so natural that your progress will be rapid.

In another few weeks you may wonder how you ever could have been so stiff and so clumsy. So remember again: the other fellow, the one who performs Jiu Jitsu so well, was once as rigid and as worried as you are now.   Cheer up, Beginner!

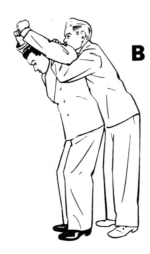

Lift both arms high and bend forward. Bring your head up sharply and bring both elbows straight down in a powerful, quick movement; and at same time drop your hips way down as shown. This entire action is done simultaneously and quickly to capitalize on the element of surprise. Opponent will be unable to hold. Keep bending forward for balance while dropping down.

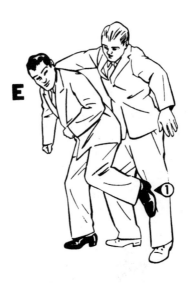

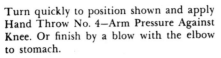

Turn quickly to position shown and apply Hand Throw No. 4—Arm Pressure Against Knee. Or finish by a blow with the elbow to stomach.

Opponent will fall.

In any case in which opponent stands behind you, a strong kick to his knee-cap with sole of foot (1)—or a kick to any part of leg front with back of heel—will not only free you, but will also cripple opponent at least temporarily, and will probably floor him.

BE CAREFUL IN PRACTICE.

COMBINATION TRICKS: Illustrations below show how to work out combinations of tricks. Obviously all possible combinations cannot be illustrated. You can make up many more. Drawings below are taken directly from tricks referred to, and should not be taken too literally when practicing. Their purpose is merely to *suggest* the action. You are supposed to *know* the tricks before trying to apply them in combination. *In fact, you cannot understand these instructions unless you have already practiced the tricks referred to.*

SPOONING ANKLE THROW— TO STRANGLE HOLD NO. 1

If you try Spooning Ankle No. 2 (Session 1), and get to position shown here and find you cannot finish . . .

THE KNEE WHIRL— TO STRANGLE HOLD NO. 2

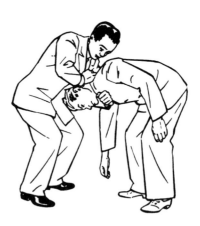

If you try The Knee Whirl (Session 2) and get opponent to point shown here, and for some reason cannot finish . . .

You can change to Strangle Hold No. 2 (Session 4) and finish as described therein.

You can change the position of your right hand from his shoulder to his wrist and go into Strangle Hold No. 1 (Session 4) and finish as described therein.

BREAKING STRANGLE HOLD— TO STRANGLE HOLD NO. 2

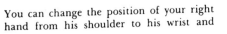

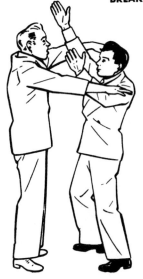

After you have broken opponent's strangle hold as shown in Breaking—Opponent Strangles from Front (Session 1) . . .

You can go into Strangle Hold No. 2 (Session 4) and finish as described therein.

Session 5.

Here in Session 5, are the following tricks:

Hand Throw No. 1 (including finishing trick)
Hand Throw No. 2 (also 1 and 2 from Sitting Position)
Hand Throw No. 3—Spinner (with finishing trick)
Defense Against Knife (finishing with Hand Throws 1 and 2)
Defense Against Knife (high blow and straight jab)
Defense Against Club
Breaking—When Opponent Holds from Rear

Hand Throw No. 1 is the famous "flip-toss"—or throw by pressure against wrist joint. Hand Throw No. 2 is especially useful in cramped quarters. It will pay you to learn both these hand throws well, as several knife and pistol tricks depend on them for success.

Because this session also gives you an effective defense against knife attack—highly practical knowledge these days—we urge you to practice this session even more diligently than usual. Some day you'll doubtless be glad you did.

Tricks that Leave Opponent Unable to Retaliate

We would like to call your attention again to the authenticity of this book. There are no fake or made-up tricks herein. This is immensely important to you. It is sad but true that the average student—unless advanced—does not know whether the trick he is so diligently studying is fake or authentic.

The unhappy revelation comes when someone hits him in the jaw as a result of the vulnerable position caused by an inefficient trick.

An authentic Jiu Jitsu trick, properly executed, should end with opponent in such a state that he will be unable to counter-attack. You will find this true of the tricks in this course. We have not wasted your time on any of the hundreds of so-called Jiu Jitsu tricks which leave you wide open at the finish.

Hand Throw No. 1

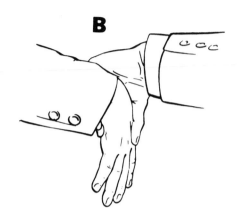

Stand just far enough away so that your hand can grasp opponent's wrist. RELAX. With your left hand turned so that the palm is outward and the thumb pointing down, reach for opponent's hand (1) on the same side (as you face him).

This shows how to grasp and hold opponent's hand (lightly) with the thumb against the back of his hand and with your four fingers encircling the base of his thumb.

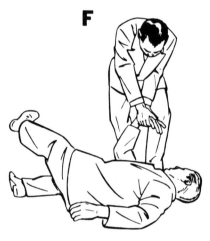

Now press his hand (with the heel of your right thumb only; left hand merely holds) toward a point just outside his right foot.

Use hand power only. Do not move shoulder. Do not bend your hips. Keep chest bent forward a little. Keep elbow low; don't stretch it out. (In practice, relax and repeat this movement several times.)
Do not twist opponent's hand too much to left or he may save himself by stepping forward.

Continue pressing until opponent is forced to ground.
Be sure to start this trick while standing almost at arms-length from opponent's shoulder. If standing too close, trick may not be effective.
The directions given are for throwing opponent to your left side. To throw to right, reverse all these instructions. Practice both sides.

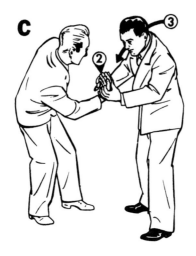

C

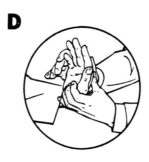

D

This shows position of hands in "C."

Imagine that his elbow is the hub of a wheel. Start drawing his hand up and around the rim of the wheel. At the same time grasp opponent's hand with your right hand (2) so that the heel of your hand is a little above opponent's wrist joint. Bring your right shoulder forward in the direction you are pressing (3) and bend body forward in the "defense" posture as shown above. Carry his hand around to the point where it normally stops. (In practice, relax and repeat this movement several times.) Hold opponent's hand lightly. Do not squeeze or use power up to this point. Now stop momentarily.

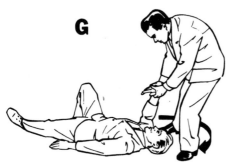

G

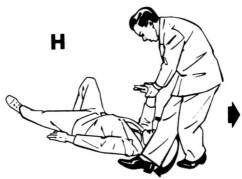

H

To finish, you can apply the Straight Arm Wrist Lock to opponent even though he is in a lying position. Without changing hands, start walking around opponent's head as shown.

Continue walking around opponent.

CONTINUED ON NEXT PAGE

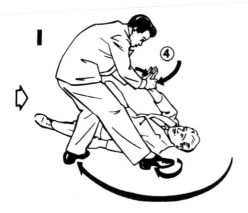

Press his hand back toward his elbow, against the wrist joint (4). This will usually hold him.

If he turns his body face downward, apply more pressure. If he continues to move his body, place your left foot on his hip.

REGARDING THE USE OF HAND THROWS

Throwing or holding opponent by twisting, bending, or stretching his joints "the wrong way," is a type of trick called "against the joint," since it involves pressure against the natural movement. Application of this type of trick not only destroys opponent's defensive power by putting him in a helpless position, or by causing him to lose his balance and to fall, but it also is extremely painful.

The joints of the fingers, hands, arms, legs, neck may all be attacked by this type of trick.

Warning: This type of trick is dangerous. So be exceedingly careful in practice. Jerking should not be used in applying the trick or in resisting it. If jerking is used, you may cause a dislocation or sprain; and, in addition, you will not improve in your efforts to master the trick. Furthermore, you lose the meaning of Jiu Jitsu, which should be soft and gentle.

Hand Throw No. 2

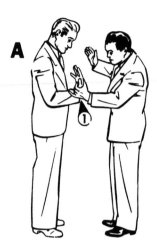

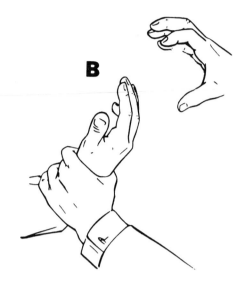

This is a good trick in many emergencies, especially in cramped quarters. Stand just far enough away so that your hand can reach opponent's wrist. RELAX. With your left hand, grasp opponent's wrist on the same side and bring up directly in front of you (1) with his fingers pointing straight up. (Important: Do not raise opponent's elbow.)

This shows position of hands in "A."

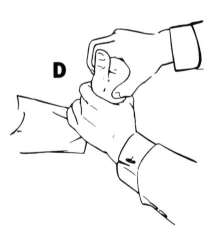

This shows position of hands in "C."

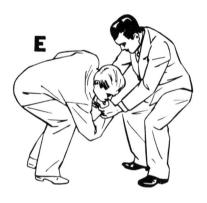

Continue pressing.

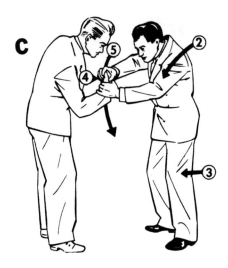

Bend forward (2). Bend your knees to "defense" posture (3). With your right hand, grasp top of opponent's fist very tightly (4). Press the heel of your right hand against his knuckles to apply pressure against wrist joint; and continue to press downward (5) using only the power in your hand. Do not raise shoulder. Keep his elbow low. Do not move your chest. Be sure opponent's elbow is a few inches away from his body, to avoid support against his body.

HAND THROWS FROM SITTING POSITION

You can throw opponent with either Hand Throw No. 1 or No. 2 when you are seated and opponent is standing. Before starting, sit forward a little in your seat. Then grasp opponent's hand as described in the instructions for these two throws. Then you will find you can continue as easily as if you were standing. If you use Hand Throw No. 1, you can stand up after opponent is down, and finish as described. If you use Hand Throw No. 2, you can remain seated and still hold opponent on his knees before you.

If you are standing and opponent is seated, you can throw him out of his seat and to the ground by using either of these two throws. If using No. 2, step back a little with both feet after grasping his hand.

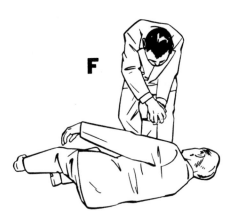

Opponent will go down in one of two ways. He may fall to side as shown. Or he may go down on one knee. In the latter case, twist his hand a little to the left and this will force him over onto his back. Then you can hold him. In close quarters—especially where there is no room for a throw—hold opponent down on his knees.

NOTE: If, in "C," opponent resists by pushing his fist upward, step back farther and pull and press his wrist downward with more power.

Practice this trick on the opposite side, reversing all instructions.

Hand Throw No. 3 – Spinner

In perfecting this trick, footwork and balance are so important that they should be practiced first. To start, stand with each foot directly underneath corresponding shoulder. Now drop a coin (1), or other marker, about 24 inches to the rear of your feet as a guide for your foot position at finish of spin.

Place hands on your legs (2), bend your knees (3), drop hips a little, and spin (4). Turning on the ball of one foot (5), spin a three-quarter turn (6). Try turning one way and then the other. Now try it with your hands off your knees. Spin several times until you can do the turn with perfect balance. Now you are ready to learn the handwork.

Extend your right arm with thumb up and reach for opponent's wrist on the opposite side (7). Your palm should face opponent's palm. Your thumb goes around his wrist joint. Now, without stopping
Push opponent's arm out about one foot as

shown (8). Do not grip his wrist too tightly. Now quickly reach out with your other hand (9) and place it on top of opponent's hand so that his hand is flat between your hands. Start your spin toward the right as shown (10).

Practice this trick from opposite side, reversing all instructions.

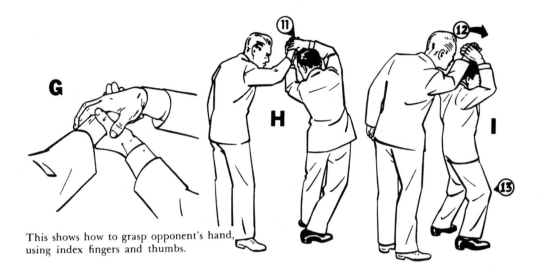

G

This shows how to grasp opponent's hand, using index fingers and thumbs.

Continue your spin, using the movement you practiced in "A," "B," and "C." When your hands swing over the top of your head (11), tighten your grasp (but not too much) on his hand.

Continue spin. As you turn, start pressing opponent's hand down (12) with your left palm (do not twist, but press down). Keep knees bent a little (13). As your hands pass over top of your head, keep them low (otherwise opponent may be able to execute a counter spin, in which case you will end up again in poition "F.")

J

Keep going . . .

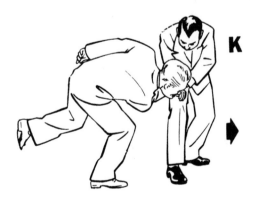

K

To a three-quarter turn.

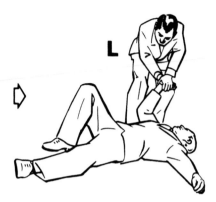

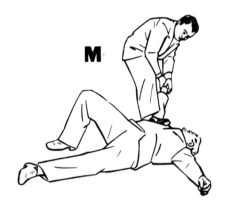

By the time you finish your spin, opponent will be on the ground, if you have executed the trick properly. This will bring you to the position shown. (If opponent is still standing after your spin, as in "J," continue pressing with left palm until he falls.) Do not hold your hands too high while he is. falling; otherwise he may be able to turn his body sidewise on the ground. However, if he does twist to the side, pull his arm toward you, forcing him to lie flat on his back.

To hold him there, place your right foot in his armpit, keep a tight grip on his hand, and press his hand toward the ground without more twisting.

Defense Against Knife

If opponent attempts to stab you with a knife from a low position as shown above (1) . . .

Bring his arm up and around (4), and continue Hand Throw No. 2.

Now you can hold him or disarm him.

B

C

Block the blow by crossing your arms (2). At the same time spread your legs, in a little jump, so that you assume position shown. Then grasp his wrist quickly with

your left hand (3). Now you can finish with Hand Throw No. 2, as shown in the following illustrations.

F

G

Again, if opponent attacks as in "A" . . .

You can block the blow as in "B" . . . and grasp his hand with your left hand, with thumb against back of his hand (5).

CONTINUED ON NEXT PAGE

If a person attacks you with a knife, it always helps to throw something in his face—handkerchief, small change, book, hat, coat, (ladies can throw their shoes, pocketbook, hat, or anything else handy) —to blind or excite opponent temporarily.

Then you can effectively kick or strike opponent in one of the vital spots.

Another effective defense: When opponent attempts to strike with knife, quickly strike his fore-arm (the one with the knife) with the side of your hand—a good, sharp blow—and this will make him drop the knife.

Now you can finish with Hand Throw No. 1. Right hand grasps his hand as shown (6).

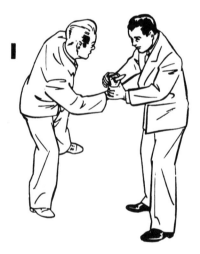

Bring his hand up and around. Continue until he is down and you can finish as shown in Hand Throw No. 1.

Defense Against Knife

A

If opponent attempts to stab you with knife, from position shown . . .

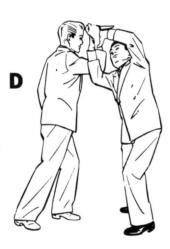

D

Proceed as described in Elbow Lock (Up).

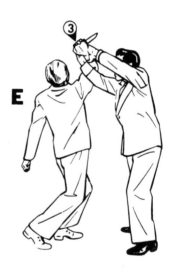

E

Now you can hold him (provided you do not pull him back so far that he falls). Change the position of your right or left hand (either one) to top of opponent's hand (3), in order to clamp the knife tightly and keep him from grabbing knife with other hand. Or you can disable him with a strong kick to the shins.

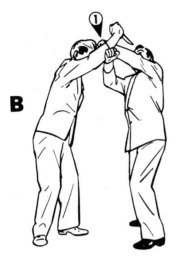

B

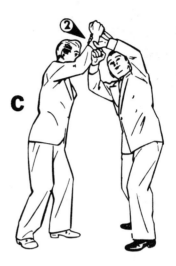

C

Cross your arms and at same time step in closer with either foot, and block blow as shown (1). Quickly seize opponent's wrist with your left hand (2). Now you are in a position to finish with Elbow Lock (Up).

If opponent attempts to stab you by a straight jab, you can defend yourself by a kick to the shins. In almost any case, a strong kick to the shins is good defense. If you happen to have a strong arm (don't try this if you haven't), you can always block opponent's blow by catching his upper arm with your hand; then you can go into any of the finishes described.

F

Breaking– Opponent Holds from Rear

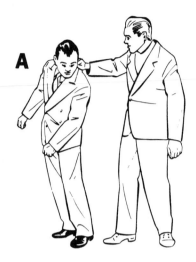

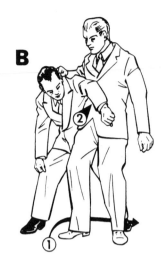

If opponent attempts to hold your collar or shoulder from rear . . .

Move behind opponent by placing your left foot behind his left foot (1). Get your hip under opponent's hip. Bend forward as shown. At same time place your left arm across his stomach, (2). Bend your knees.

NOTE: This trick seems at first to need considerable strength, but practice shows that your hip acts as a fulcrum over which you tilt opponent.

Another way to throw opponent from position shown in "C": As you lift up with right hand swing your upper body to left. This will cause opponent to fall to your rear.

If opponent attempts to choke or hold from rear as in "A," you can free self by a blow with your elbow to the solar plexus, stomach, or short ribs.

Or, you can also free self by swinging your shoulder around (in either direction), striking his arm with the corner of the shoulder.

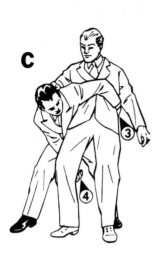

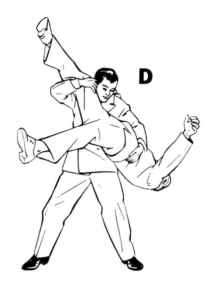

Left hand encircles opponent's waist (3) and pulls him in close to your side as shown. Right hand now grasps opponent's right leg from behind (4). Knees are still bent.

Now, in one motion, straighten up your knees and your back; lift up with your right hand and push back with your left elbow. This will lift opponent with his weight on your hip as shown. Drop him.

Defense Against Club

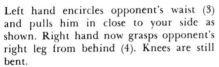

If you face a person who attempts to strike you on the head with a club, you can break the blow and finish exactly as described in the knife-defense—finishing with Elbow Lock (Up).

Also, if you face an opponent armed with a club raised high . . .

You can dive against his knees as shown. This will throw him as illustrated, and most likely will disable his knee at the same time.

Rise up quickly; this will force opponent either to fall to his side, or smash his face against ground, or do a somersault.

COMBINATION TRICKS: Illustrations below show how to work out combinations of tricks. Obviously all possible combinations cannot be illustrated. You can make up many more. Drawings below are taken directly from tricks referred to, and should not be taken too literally when practicing. Their purpose is merely to *suggest* the action. You are supposed to *know* the tricks before trying to apply them in combination. *In fact, you cannot understand these instructions unless you have already practiced the tricks referred to.*

WHEN OPPONENT RESISTS SWEEPING CALF NO. 2 BY STEPPING BACK

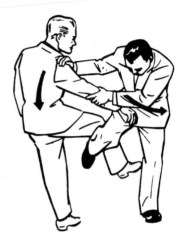

If you try Sweeping Calf No. 2 (Session 1) and opponent refuses to step into position shown here, but steps back with his right foot in order to resist . . .

Keep pulling with your left hand and follow his movement by sliding your feet forward and you will find yourself in the right position to continue the tricks as if he had not resisted.

Or, instead of following his movement, you can release your left hand and apply Hand Throw No. 4 (Session 3) against his left knee.

SWEEPING CALF NO. 2— TO SPRING HIP THROW

If you attempt Sweeping Calf No. 2 (Session 1) and opponent refuses to step into position shown here, but steps back with his right leg in order to resist . . .

You can go into Spring Hip Throw (Session 2), or Sweeping-Side Hip Throw (Session 3).

122

WHEN OPPONENT RESISTS SPOONING ANKLE NO. 1 BY STEPPING BACK

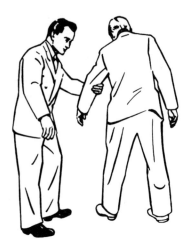

If you attempt Spooning Ankle No. 1 (Session 1) and opponent refuses to step into position shown here but steps back with his left foot in order to resist . . .

Bring your right hand around and grasp his left hand and go into Hand Throw No. 1 (Session 5).

WHEN OPPONENT RESISTS THE KNEE WHIRL

If you attempt The Knee Whirl (Session 2) and opponent succeeds in resisting at this point . . .

You can resume your original position and immediately start The Knee Whirl again. But remember, when you come back to original position, be sure your balance is solid and strong before starting again. This is one of the few tricks in Jiu Jitsu which can be used in combination with itself . . . one at which you can usually succeed by repeating.

Session 6.

containing:

Arm Lock No. 1
Breaking—Opponent Holds Arms
Breaking—Opponent Holds from Front
Breaking—Opponent Holds Two Hands from Rear
Breaking—Opponent Holds Arms from Front
Breaking—Opponent Hugs from Rear, Over Arms
Breaking—Opponent Holds Arms from Front
Hand Throw No. 2 to Strangle Hold
Elbow Lock (Down) to Sweeping Calf
Hand Throw No. 1 to Hand Throw No. 4
Hand Throw No. 1 to Sweeping Calf
Elbow Lock (Up) to Sweeping Calf

Arm Lock No. 1

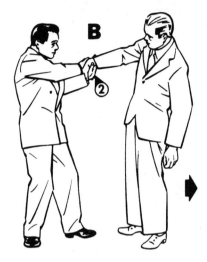

With your right hand, grasp opponent's right hand (1) as shown (thumb on back of opponent's hand, fingers inside palm).

Lift opponent's hand to point shown and grasp his wrist in the "V" between thumb and forefinger of your left hand (2), with your fingers outside.

Breaking— Opponent Holds Arms

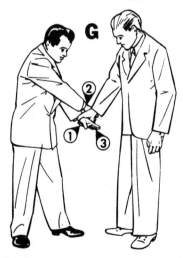

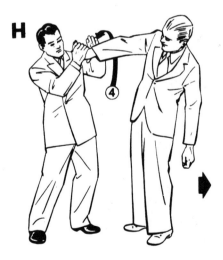

If opponent attempts to hold your left hand with his right hand (1), or with his two hands, grasp his right hand with your right hand (2), with all five fingers over top of his hand and with tips of your fingers wrapped around edge of opponent's hand. Spread the thumb and fore-fingers of your left hand to make a "V" as shown (3).

Bring your left fingers up and catch his wrist in the "V" of your left hand and turn his arm and bring it down to your front, as shown (4). Note how your right hand holds opponent's hand.

C

D

Step with your left foot to a point just in front of opponent's left foot (3). Let your right foot turn naturally to follow this movement (4). At same time, turn opponent's arm until you have it in position shown (5).

Keep holding his hand with your two hands. Place your left forearm on top of his elbow and press down (6).

Breaking –

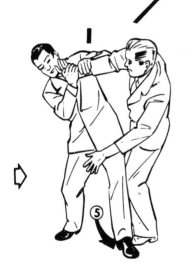

I

J

Swing your left foot over to a point just in front of opponent's left foot (5). Continue as in "D" and "E" above. Now finish as in "F."

If opponent attempts to strangle with two hands from the side, grasp his right hand with your right hand (1), with all five fingers over top of his hand, and grasp his right wrist in the "V" of your left hand.

E **F**

Drop shoulder so that elbow power comes from shoulder. Shift your weight to your left leg. Keep pressing against his elbow and hold him. To punish opponent more, let your right hand press the back of opponent's hand toward his elbow.

KNOCK-OUT FINISH (if necessary): "F" is a good position from which to start knock-out blow to his ribs with your left elbow.

The three breaking tricks below show practical applications of this arm lock.

Keep pressing with your elbow. Bend your body toward his shoulder, and bend your left knee (7).

Turn back to page 127 for steps G and H

Opponent Holds from Front

K

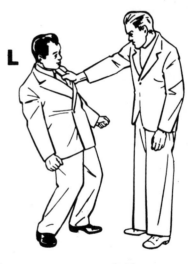

L

Swing your left foot to the right to a point just in front of opponent's left foot, while you turn his arm (using only hand power) and bring it down to your front. Finish as in "F" above.

If opponent strangles with left hand in front and right hand back of your neck, or comes in very close, push his nose with the palm of your free hand. This will force him back and put you in position to start as in "J."

If opponent attempts to hold your coat or shirt with his right arm straight out, grasp his right hand with your right hand, with all five fingers over top of his hand, and his right wrist with your left hand, exactly as in "J." Continue as in "C," "D," "E" and "F."

The tricks on this page all use the same basic movement, starting from different positions.

If any difficulty is encountered, a strong kick against opponent's shin will help you get started.

Breaking– Opponent Holds Two Hands from Rear

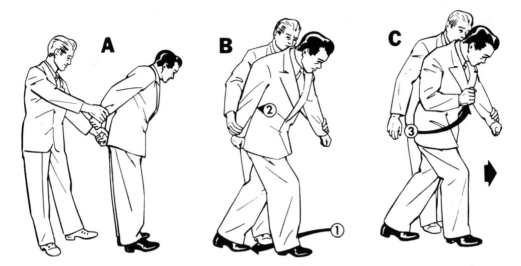

If opponent attempts to hold both hands from rear as shown . . .

Move your left foot to outside of his right foot as shown (1), keeping your chest facing original direction. Do not turn. Important —don't try to break his hold at this point or you will lose him. Keep right elbow close to ribs (2).

Now break grip of his right hand by lifting your right fist up sharply (3).

Or from position shown in "D" you can finish by a sharp blow with elbow to his solar plexus or short ribs.

You can also free yourself from this hold (from position "A") by stepping back closer to opponent and delivering a powerful kick to his knee with the sole of your foot.

If opponent holds your arms higher than shown in these pictures, the movements described are even easier to do.

Another break for position shown in "A": Keep elbows close to body. Bend forward. Now bring both fists up sharply. Opponent will be unable to hold.

Remember that these illustrations show slow motion action. Your movements, in an emergency, must be done with flashing speed. Practice again and again until you achieve this speed.

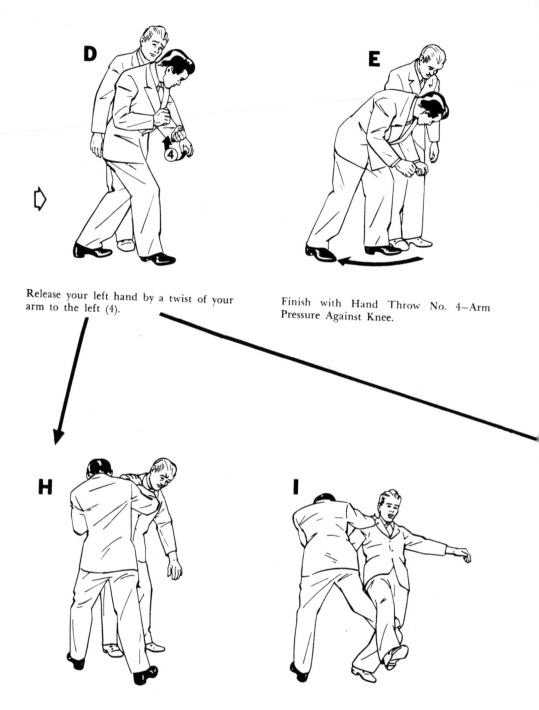

D

Release your left hand by a twist of your arm to the left (4).

E

Finish with Hand Throw No. 4—Arm Pressure Against Knee.

H

Or from position shown in "D" you can finish by turning your body quickly to left and applying Sweeping Calf.

I

This shows continuation of Sweeping Calf.

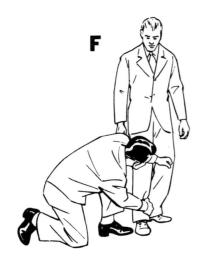

This and following picture show finish with Hand Throw No. 4.

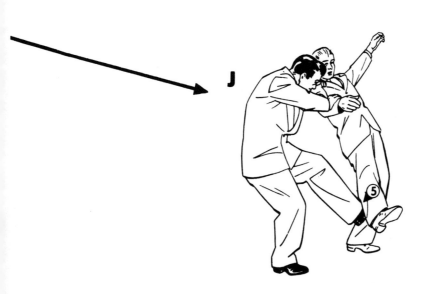

Or from position shown in "D" you can finish by Spooning Ankle Throw, applying your left foot against his right ankle as shown (5).

Breaking- Opponent Holds Arms from Front

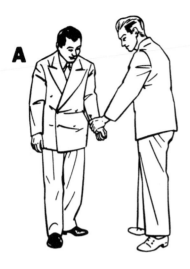

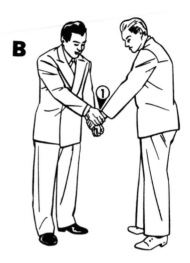

If opponent attempts to hold your left arm with his left hand . . .

Grasp opponent's left hand with your right hand (1) so that your thumb and forefinger circle his hand just below wrist joint.

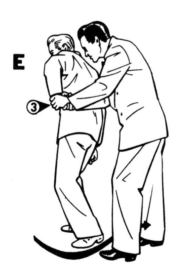

. . . until this position is reached. Now grasp his left hand with your left (3), releasing your right. You can finish with Strangle Hold No. 1, or with Arm Lock No. 1, Shoulder Lock, or Elbow Lock (Down) No. 1.

If opponent attempts to hold your left hand with both hands . . .

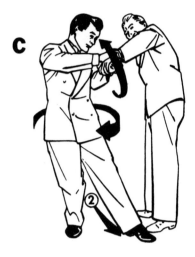

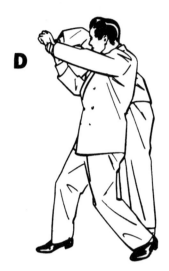

Spin to right, leading off with your left foot (2), exactly as described in Strangle Hold No. 1 (from Rear), and keep going

. . . in one continuous motion . . .

Grasp opponent's left hand with your right hand as described in "B" and start spinning to right disregarding his right hand which will lose its grasp automatically as you turn.

Continue as in "D" and "E."
Be sure to try every trick from opposite side, reversing all directions.

Breaking –

Opponent Hugs from Rear,

Over Arms

A

If opponent attempts to hug tightly from rear, over arms . . . Bend forward in "defense" posture. Press your hips closely against his front. Keep this position throughout this trick.

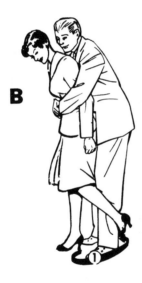

B

Now hook your left foot behind opponent's left ankle (1).

C

Now quickly kick opponent's ankle UP as high as possible, putting as much power as you can into your toes (2). Apply all possible power against opponent's leg at the point of contact with the top of your foot.

If opponent holds from rear with an arm lock and steps back a little, you can free yourself by moving back closer to opponent which will put you in position to execute "B" and "C."

You can also break the hold shown above by a powerful kickback to opponent's knee-cap, or shin, with the sole of your foot.

You can also free yourself by a sharp blow with the back of your head to his chin. If opponent is too short for a blow to his chin, the same blow to his nose or forehead will be equally effective.

Breaking– Opponent Holds Arms from Front

OR →

If opponent attempts to hold your two arms with his two hands as shown . . .

Or if he attempts to hold your left wrist with his right hand as shown . . .

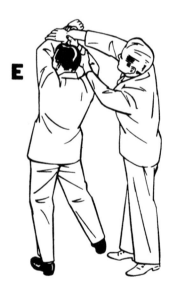

This and the next picture show continuation as in Strangle Hold No. 1.

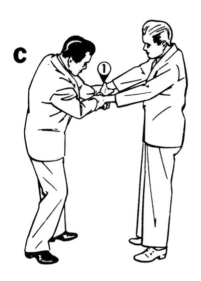

C

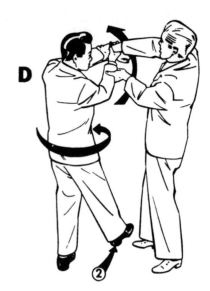

D

Grasp his right wrist with your right hand (1), so that the palm of your hand is inside his wrist and your thumb is at the back of his hand just below wrist joint.

Lead off with your right foot (2) and, without stopping, turn to left and continue as shown in Strangle Hold No. 1—from Rear. NOTE: In grasping his right wrist with your right hand, it is preferable to start a swinging motion, the impetus of which carries straight through as you spin around.

At this point you can change, if you wish, to Arm Lock No. 1 (in which case you can press against his elbow joint with your left elbow, OR with your left hand). Or you can release your hold and go into Shoulder Lock or Elbow Lock (Down) No. 1.

G

CONTINUED ON NEXT PAGE

143

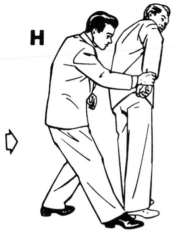

This and following two pictures show finish as in Strangle Hold No. 1.

OR➔

Arms all the way around neck.

Hand Throw No. 2 to Strangle Hold

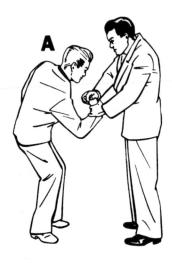

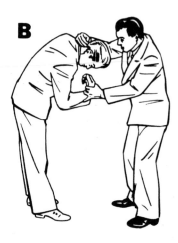

If you succeed in getting opponent to position above, using Hand Throw No. 2—

No matter whether he resists or not, you can suddenly change to a Strangle Hold. Place hand (the one which was on top in previous picture) behind opponent's neck and pull his head forward and down as shown.

Hand Throw No. 1 to Sweeping Calf

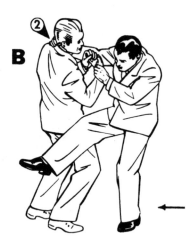

If you apply Hand Throw No. 1 and opponent attempts to resist by grasping his captured hand with his free hand (1), or by pulling his hand back, or by any other action, you can then proceed with Sweeping Calf.

Step forward with your left foot. Free your right hand and place it against opponent's left shoulder (2). At same time sweep opponent's right leg with your right leg exactly as explained in Sweeping Calf.

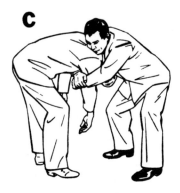

C

Regarding Combination Tricks

Combinations (or changes from one trick to another) are important. You may occasionally start a trick and find that for some reason you cannot finish it. By resisting your initial action, your opponent will always provide the opportunity for still another trick. Obviously, combination tricks are more difficult to resist, and are therefore more effective. Here are a few examples of logical combinations. You will be able to work out many other combinations with practice.

Now you can proceed with Strangle Hold No. 2, or with the hold shown above (a slight variation) in which your arms encircle one of opponent's arms as well as his neck.

Elbow Lock (Up) to Sweeping Calf

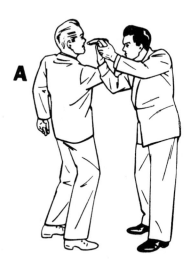

A

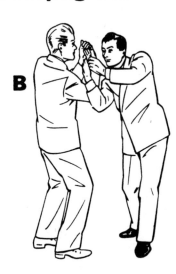

B

If you succeed in getting opponent's arm to position shown above, using Elbow Lock (Up). . . .

And if opponent resists by grasping his captured arm with his free hand, or by any other method . . . you can still throw him by suddenly changing to Sweeping Calf.

147

Hand Throw No. 1 to Hand Throw No. 4

If you apply Hand Throw No. 1 and get opponent's hand to position shown above. . . .

You can immediately go into Hand Throw No. 4 by dropping to your knees and applying your left arm against opponent's left knee, as explained in detail under Hand Throw No. 4. Note that if you apply Hand Throw No. 1 to opponent's RIGHT hand, you must apply Hand Throw No. 4 to LEFT leg, and vice versa.

Elbow Lock (Down) to Sweeping Calf

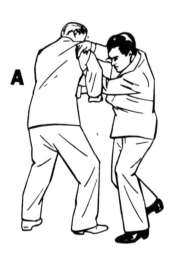

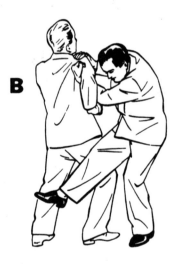

If you start to apply Elbow Lock (Down) and opponent resists by grasping his captured arm with his free hand, or by pulling back, stop his action momentarily at the point shown above (to strengthen your balance).

Now you can defeat him by suddenly changing to Sweeping Calf.

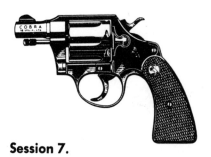

Session 7.

Defending Yourself Against a Pistol

Defense Against Pistol No. 1

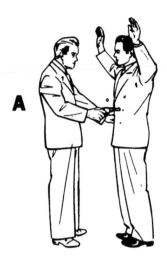

If opponent points pistol at you from directly in front, from front left side, or from front right side, raise hands to HEAD height. RELAX.

Using the hand on same side as gun (that is, your left if opponent holds gun in his right as above), go into the following action:

REGARDING DEFENSE AGAINST PISTOL

If opponent points pistol and threatens to shoot, you can overcome him, defeat the weapon, and remove yourself from danger by one of the tricks on these pages.

Regardless of whether opponent points pistol at you from front, side, or back, and regardless of type of gun used, these tricks are effective, *so long as opponent or gun is within reach.*

But remember:

1. When a gun is pointed at you, put up your hands, even if not told to do so. By your willing submission, put opponent's mind at ease.

2. Act with utmost discretion. Make no move which is likely to excite opponent or to suggest that you may be looking for an opening.

3. Don't hurry. Patiently await your opportunity. He will probably step closer. When he does, this is the time to act.

All movements at same time } Quickly (with the same speed you would employ to catch a mosquito in flight) catch his gun hand and shove it across your front and down as shown (1). Your grasp should be tight so that his hand cannot be jerked away. Slide right foot back (2), holding weight on left foot, in order to get right leg out of line of fire.

By keeping your weight on your left foot, you can move your right foot more quickly out of line of fire, maintain better balance and greater strength. Do not look directly at gun before starting, as this may warn him. Do not hit his hand too hard or he may drop gun. And do not bend your body too much (see above).

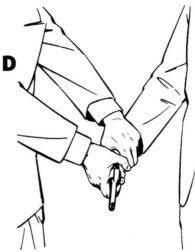

Now place your free hand against side of gun as shown (3), in preparation for the throw. Hand must hold gun and opponent's fingers at same time. In moving this hand down into position, do not pass it in front of gun.

This shows how hands hold opponent's hand and gun in "C" (viewed from opposite side).

If opponent backs you against a wall and orders either hands up or hands down, it will be still easier to shove pistol aside since you have greater strength (with the wall re-inforcing your balance); and it is unnecessary to step back with either foot. PRACTICE THIS TRICK FROM OPPOSITE SIDE, reversing all instructions.

Some students find that the defense against pistol can be executed even more swiftly by using Hand Throw No. 2, after you have shoved gun aside as shown in "B" and "C." Practice Hand Throw No. 2 in this way!

It may happen that in shoving gun aside you will accidentally catch opponent's gun with your hand underneath his hand instead of above. While the position shown in "C" is preferable, trick can be finished with your hand in the under position if your other hand is brought around very quickly, since you cannot continue to hold his gun hand very long otherwise.

Remember that cool and quick action is essential.

In practice, arm opponent with toy gun. You will see that your initial action is always finished before opponent can pull trigger. If opponent DOES pull the trigger, it will be AFTER you are out of the line of fire.

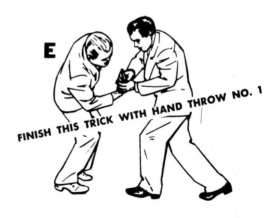

FINISH THIS TRICK WITH HAND THROW NO. 1

Now throw opponent with Hand Throw No. 1. After opponent is down, you can finish by a hard kick to his lower side ribs (striking with top part of foot rather than with point of toe).

If opponent commands you to keep hands down, this trick can be done just as easily as with hands up. Shove gun quickly aside by exactly the same movement as in "B" and the trick can be finished as explained in "E." Practice this!

Defense Against Pistol No. 2

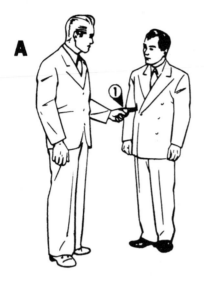

If opponent orders you to stand, HANDS DOWN, and points pistol IN HIS LEFT HAND at your RIGHT FRONT, close to arms as shown (1) . . .

Step in quickly with your right foot as shown (2). At the same instant, turn your body to left as shown and push opponent's gun and hand away with your right forearm, and bring your left hand around and catch opponent's gun and hand underneath as shown (3). Special note: Do not push against opponent too hard or he may step back; use just enough power to move gunhand away.

If opponent points pistol at your RIGHT FRONT as shown in "A," but holds gun IN HIS RIGHT HAND instead of his left, follow the instruction given in Defense Against Pistol No. 1 (above), finishing with Hand Throw No. 1, throwing to your left.

Practice the foregoing from both the left AND right front, with opponent holding pistol alternately in left AND right hand.

SPECIAL NOTE: If opponent holds gun IN HIS RIGHT HAND and points gun at your EXTREME RIGHT SIDE, and your HANDS ARE DOWN . . .

Quickly raise your right hand high, and at the same time bring your left hand across and push his gun away and proceed exactly as described in Defense Against Pistol No. 1 (above). Practice trick from both sides.

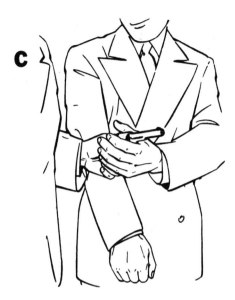

C

This shows close-up of position in "B."
Note how your left hand holds both gun
and hand at same time.

D

Now bring your right hand up and grasp
top of opponent's wrist as shown (4).

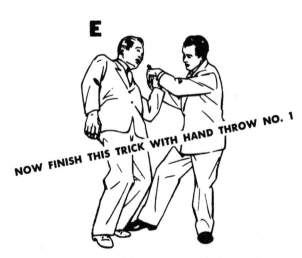

E

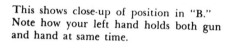

NOW FINISH THIS TRICK WITH HAND THROW NO. 1

Now without stopping, finish with Hand
Throw No. 1.

Defense Against Pistol No. 3

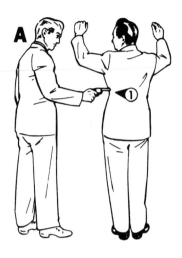

If opponent orders you to stand, HANDS UP, and points pistol IN HIS RIGHT HAND at your EXTREME LEFT SIDE (1) . . .

Swing your left arm down and to rear as shown (2), striking his gun hand with outside of your wrist (keep fist closed). At same time, step directly in front of his left foot (3) and swing your hips around and back (4) so gun won't catch in clothes. Bring your right hand around and grasp his right wrist as shown (5). Practice these movements many times, until all this can be done in one simultaneous action.

Defense Against

Pistol No. 4

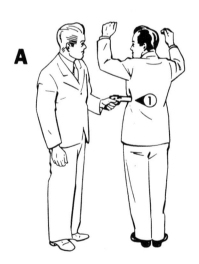

If opponent orders you to stand, HANDS UP, and points pistol IN HIS LEFT HAND at your EXTREME LEFT SIDE (1) . . .

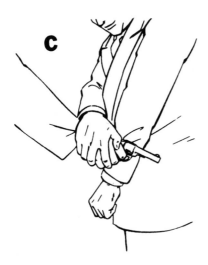

C

Close-up of position in "B." Important: Hold his hand and gun very close to your body.

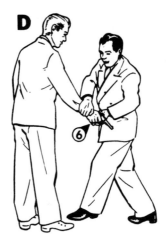

D

Now your left hand grasps under-side of opponent's right hand (6), as shown. (Be sure to grasp both gun AND fingers at same time.)

CONTINUED ON NEXT PAGE

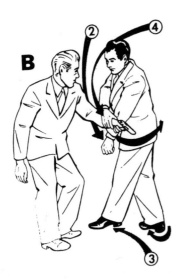

B

Swing your left arm down and to rear, shoving gun aside (2). At same time, step forward with left foot as shown (3). Swing your hips around and back. Bring right arm over and grasp opponent's wrist (4).

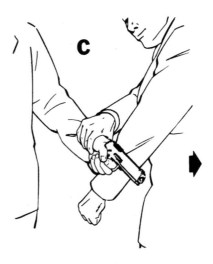

C

Close-up of position in "B." Be sure gun is pointing away from body as shown.

CONTINUED ON NEXT PAGE

Defense Against Pistol No. 3

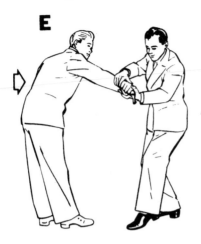

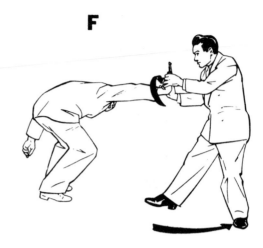

Finish with Straight-Arm Wrist Lock.

This shows finish with Straight-Arm Wrist Lock. Step back with one or both feet and turn opponent's wrist clockwise.

If opponent points gun IN HIS RIGHT HAND at your RIGHT SIDE (instead of left as in the foregoing), follow the action described in the trick below, finishing with Hand Throw No. 1.

Defense Against Pistol No. 4

FINISH THIS TRICK WITH HAND THROW NO. 1

Now your left hand grasps under-side of opponent's left hand (5). Be sure to grasp both gun AND fingers at the same time.

Finish with Hand Throw No. 1.

If opponent points gun IN HIS LEFT HAND at your RIGHT SIDE (instead of left as in the foregoing), follow the action described in the trick above, finishing with Straight-Arm Wrist Lock.

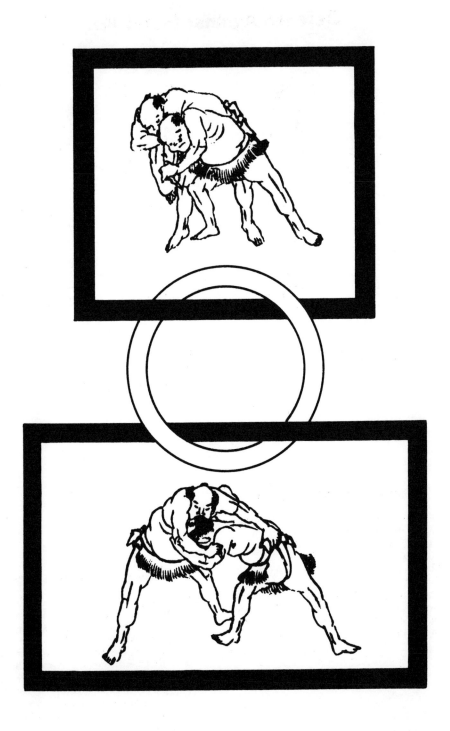

Defense Against Pistol No. 5

A

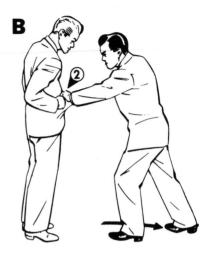

B

If opponent holds pistol in coat pocket (1), and orders hands up or hands down . . .

Seize top of his hand and gun (of course while it is still in coat), and push his hand and gun against his stomach (2). Step back with your right leg, as shown, to keep it out of possible line of fire.

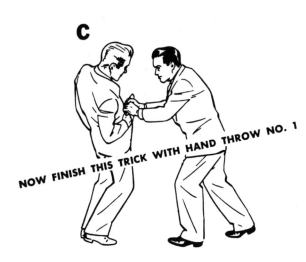

C

NOW FINISH THIS TRICK WITH HAND THROW NO. 1

Now, without stopping, finish with Hand Throw No. 1.

D

Or you can finish by a blow to a vital spot.

E

Illustration of finish by blow to side of head with edge of hand.

Defense Against Pistol No. 6

 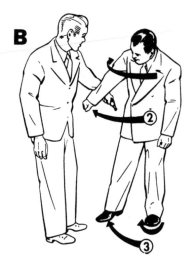

If opponent orders you to stand with HANDS DOWN OR UP, and points pistol IN HIS LEFT HAND at you from rear (1) . . . (Before starting this trick, be sure you feel gun in your back.)

You can turn either to left or right, but if you desire to make a RIGHT turn, swing your right hand down and around to rear, shoving gun aside as shown (2). At same time, step back with your right foot (3). NOTE direction in which feet are now pointing.

Defense Against Pistol No. 7

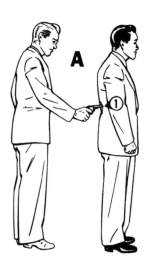 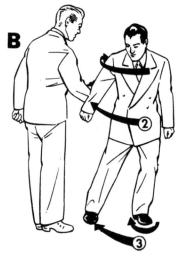

If opponent orders you to stand with HANDS DOWN OR UP, and points pistol IN HIS RIGHT HAND at you from rear (1) . . . (Again be sure you feel gun in your back.)

You can turn either to right or left, but if you desire to make a RIGHT turn, swing your right hand to rear (2), shoving gun aside as shown. At the same time, step back with your right foot (3).

C

D

Quickly bring your left hand around and grasp wrist of his gun hand (4).

Now your right hand grasps under-side of opponent's left hand (5). Be sure to grasp both gun AND fingers at same time.

CONTINUED ON NEXT PAGE

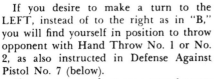

If you desire to make a turn to the LEFT, instead of to the right as in "B," you will find yourself in position to throw opponent with Hand Throw No. 1 or No. 2, as also instructed in Defense Against Pistol No. 7 (below).

If opponent stands at your rear, be very sure that gun is close enough to your body to be felt. Don't take chances. Opponent must be near enough for you to be able to grab the gun.

These descriptions assume that opponent holds gun at your rear near your waist. If he holds the gun higher, the trick is still easier to execute.

C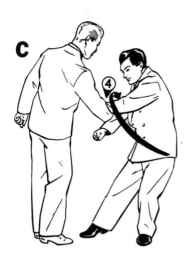

D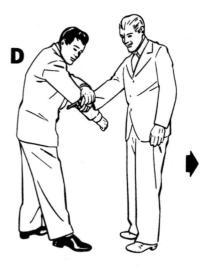

Quickly bring your left hand around and grasp wrist of his gun hand (4).

Close-up of position "C," viewed from opposite side. CONTINUED ON NEXT PAGE

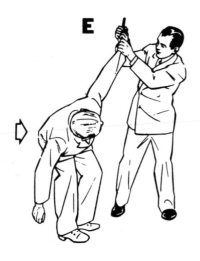

Bring his hand up and around (6) and finish with Arm Lock No. 1, or Straight-Arm Wrist Lock as instructed in Defense Against Pistol No. 3.

This shows finish, using Arm Lock No. 1.

Defense Against Pistol No. 6

Defense Against Pistol No. 7

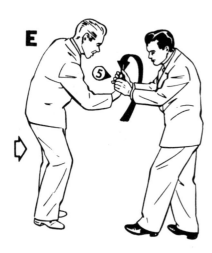

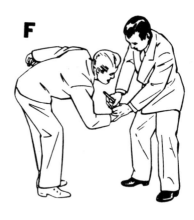

This shows finish with Hand Throw No. 2.

Now your right hand grasps under-side of opponent's gun hand (5). Be sure to grasp both gun AND fingers at same time. Now bring his hand up and around and finish with Hand Throw No. 1 or No. 2.

If you desire to make a turn to the LEFT, instead of to the right as in "B," you will find yourself in position to throw opponent with Arm Lock No. 1, or Straight-Arm Wrist Lock, as also instructed in Defense Against Pistol No. 6 (above).

COMBINATION TRICKS: Illustrations below show how to work out combinations of tricks. Obviously all possible combinations cannot be illustrated. You can make up many more. Drawings below are taken directly from tricks referred to, and should not be taken too literally when practicing.

Their purpose is merely to *suggest* the action. You are supposed to *know* the tricks before trying to apply them in combination. *In fact, you cannot understand these instructions unless you have already practiced the tricks referred to.*

STRANGLE HOLD NO. 1— TO ARM LOCK

If you get opponent to position shown here in Strangle Hold No. 1 (Session 4) . . .

You can change, if you wish, to Arm Lock No. 1 (Session 6) or to almost any of the arm locks shown in this course.

BREAKING WRIST HOLD— TO STRANGLE HOLD NO. 2

After you have broken opponent's hold as shown in Breaking Wrist Hold (Session 2) . . .

You can go into Strangle Hold No. 2 (Session 4) and finish as described therein.

ARM LOCK TO STRANGLE HOLD NO. 2

If you get opponent to position shown here (finish of Defense Against Blow with Fist, Session 3), and want to change to a still stronger finish . . .

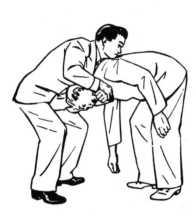

You can change to Strangle Hold No. 2 (Session 4) and finish as described therein. In this case, release your hand hold, and step around to front of opponent quickly before he can get his body into an erect position.

BREAKING WRIST HOLD— TO HAND THROW NO. 3

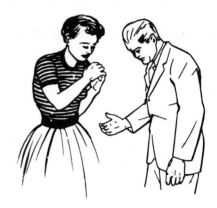

After you have broken opponent's hold as shown in Breaking Wrist Hold (Session 2) . . .

You can grasp opponent's right hand and go into Hand Throw No. 3—Spinner (Session 5) and finish as described therein.

COMBINATION TRICKS: Illustrations below show how to work out combinations of tricks. Obviously all possible combinations cannot be illustrated. You can make up many more. Drawings below are taken directly from tricks referred to, and should not be taken too literally when practicing.

Their purpose is merely to *suggest* the action. You are supposed to *know* the tricks before trying to apply them in combination. *In fact, you cannot understand these instructions unless you have already practiced the tricks referred to.*

DEFENSE AGAINST CLUB

If opponent attempts to strike you with club as shown (from Defense Against Club, Session 5) . . . or with knife (as shown in Defense Against Knife, Session 5) . . .

You can block his arms with your hands, and go into The Knee Whirl (Session 2) . . . or into Sweeping Calf No. 1 (Session 1).

HAND THROW NO. 3—SPINNER TO SWEEPING CALF NO. 1

If you try Hand Throw No. 3—Spinner (Session 5) and get opponent to this position and find you cannot finish . . .

You can immediately change to Sweeping Calf No. 1 (Session 1) and finish as described therein.

HAND THROW—TO HIP THROW

If you start Hand Throw No. 1 or Hand Throw No. 2 (Session 5) . . .

You can change (whether opponent resists or not) to Spring Hip Throw (Session 2) and finish as described therein.

Combinations (or changes from one trick to another) are important. You may occasionally start a trick and find that for some **reason** you cannot finish it. By resisting your initial action, your opponent will always provide the opportunity for still another trick. Obviously, combination tricks are more difficult to resist, and are therefore more effective. Here are a few examples of logical combinations. You will be able to work out many other combinations with practice.

ARM LOCK NO. 1— TO SPOONING ANKLE OR STRANGLE HOLD

If you get opponent to this position in Arm Lock No. 1 (Session 6) . . .

Whether he resists or not, you can change to Spooning Ankle Throw (Session 1) . . . or to Strangle Hold No. 2—from Front (Session 4).

STRANGLE HOLD NO. 1— TO SWEEPING CALF NO. 2

If you get to this point in applying Strangle Hold No. 1 (the picture above is position "G" from Breaking—Opponent Holds Arms from Front, Session 6), and if opponent resists by pulling back . . .

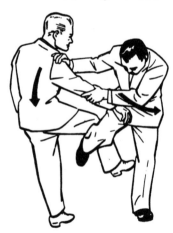

You can change the position of your hands, turn your body to opposite direction and apply Sweeping Calf No. 2 (Session 1).

HAND THROW NO. 3—SPINNER TO STRANGLE HOLD NO. 1

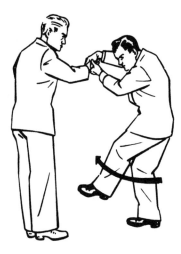

If you attempt Hand Throw No. 3—Spinner (Session 5) and get to this position and find that for some reason you cannot finish . . .

You can immediately change to Strangle Hold No. 1 (Session 4), reversing your direction and going under opponent's arms as shown. Then you can finish with Strangle Hold No. 1 or Arm Lock No. 1 (Session 6).

BREAKING FIST BLOW— TO HAND THROW NO. 3

If opponent attempts to strike you with fist and you block the blow by throwing both hands inside and against opponent's arms (from Defense Against Blow with Fist, Session 2) . . .

You can grasp opponent's hand (must be done very quickly) and go into Hand Throw No. 3—Spinner (Session 5) and finish as described therein.

Session 8.

ARTS FOR EMERGENCIES

RESUSCITATION

Resuscitation

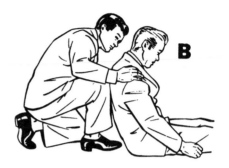

For the FIRST METHOD of reviving a person who is unconscious from strangulation, or from a blow to almost any part of the body, or from a heavy fall . . . lift patient to sitting position.

Brace your right knee against his spine.

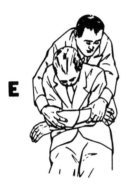

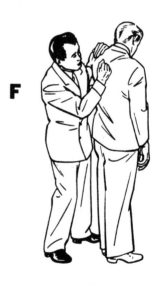

From position shown in "B," you can also go into position shown above, for the SECOND METHOD. Cross opponent's arms in front of chest. Hold the top arm as shown. Brace your knee against his spine. Now press—or squeeze—his chest against your knee, forcing the air out of his chest. Then suddenly release the pressure to allow chest to expand and draw in more air. Continue this pumping at the rate of normal breathing. Stop as soon as patient starts breathing. Then pound about ten times between shoulder blades with heel of your fist as shown in "F."

The principal difference between the first and second methods described is this: The first method helps to restore heart action as well as breathing. The second method is primarily to start breathing action.

This shows how and where to pound (easily) between shoulder blades—whether in sitting or standing position—as described in the foregoing.

172

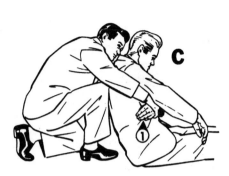

C

D

Bring his left hand over and across his chest and under his right arm (1).

Hold his left shoulder lightly with your left hand (2), and pull with your right hand to force the air out of his chest. Then suddenly release the pressure to allow chest to expand and draw in more air. Continue this pumping at the rate of normal breathing. Stop as soon as patient starts breathing. Naturally it may require only one such contraction and release. Frequently two will do the trick. Or, if the person has been "out" for some time, it may require as many as thirty such movements. After patient starts breathing, pound him about ten times between the shoulder blades with the heel (softest part) of your half closed, loosely-held fist. This stimulates nervous action.

RESUSCITATION

Resuscitation means to bring back to life, back to the senses, back to consciousness.

There are scores of resuscitation methods for all types of emergencies. Only a few are explained here, but they are simple and are sufficient for most needs.

The three requirements for success in this work are:

Proper treatment—which comes from study.

Coolness—which comes from understanding proper treatment and knowing that the method is correct.

Confidence—which comes from practice.

A few points to remember are:
WHEN YOU TREAT A PATIENT WITH ONE METHOD AND IT DOES NOT SEEM TO SUCCEED, TRY ANOTHER METHOD AND CONTINUE WORKING UNTIL YOU DO SUCCEED.

Do not give patient water while unconscious; afterwards he can have all the water he wants.

See Next Page

G

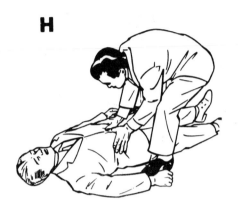

H

For the THIRD METHOD of reviving a person knocked out by a blow, fall or strangulation, stand behind patient, as closely as possible. Clasp your hands in front of patient, over his diaphragm, just below his ribs. With a quick spring-like motion, squeeze opponent's diaphragm and then release pressure.

This helps to restore breathing, and stimulates heart action. Keep up this motion until patient revives. Then pound as in "F." This method is equally effective from a sitting position.

For the FOURTH METHOD of resuscitation, place opponent flat on his back. Place your hands, spread out as shown, just below ribs. Stand as shown. Now with a quick motion slide your hands up, to force out the air; then quickly release the pressure to permit chest to expand and draw in more air Do not use to much strength; only enough to force out the air. Continue this action at rate of normal breathing until patient starts breathing naturally. Then *sit* patient upright and pound as in "F." You can also kneel on one knee, if this is more comfortable.

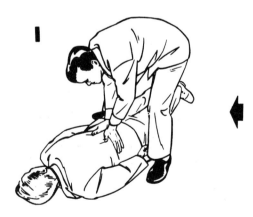

I

For the FIFTH METHOD, place patient chest down with face to side. Stand as shown. Place your hands against patient's back, about half-way down. Now with a quick spring-like motion, press straight down, forcing out the air, and then suddenly release pressure allowing chest to draw in more air. Continue this action at normal rate of breathing until natural breathing starts. Then sit patient upright and pound as in "F."

NOTE: The pressure in "H" is upward, that is, forward toward the shoulders. In "I," the pressure is exerted straight down.

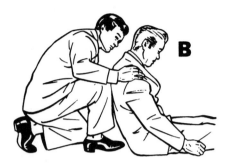

B

The following (SIXTH METHOD) is primarily for reviving a person who has been knocked out by a blow to the head. Sit patient upright as shown in "B." Place the four fingers of your right hand against patient's right temple, and the fingers of your left against his left temple. Place your right thumb against the hollow space at the back side of his neck just behind the ear and just below the base of the skull. Place your left thumb in similar position at back left side of neck. Now, in a sort of kneading action, massage his temples and the back of his neck by revolving your fingers and thumbs three times in a circular motion with medium pressure. Next, lift up his head (with a little more pressure) as if you were trying to lift his head off his body. Then, suddenly take away all pressure by removing your hands from his head. Repeat a few times. When patient revives, pound as in "F." If he does not seem to respond, shift to one of the other methods described.

The SEVENTH METHOD is for reviving a patient who has been knocked out or injured by a blow to the testes. Sit patient upright with his arm around your neck for support. Your left arm also supports patient from other side. Place your right hand against his lower abdomen (on either side but preferably in the center to make sure that you work to relieve whichever side is affected). Now quickly slide your hand downward several times for the purpose of replacing the testes in their normal position. Usually this will revive patient, but if he remains unconscious, switch to one of the other methods.

Another method of replacing testes if patient can be held up, is to pound several times as in "F," but against lower part of spine.

If you should be injured by a blow to testes, and there is no one to assist you, it will be necessary for you to jump up and down, landing each time solidly on the soles of your feet. Purpose is to jolt the testes down into normal position. Since you will be in intense pain, this requires determination—but it is an effective remedy.

J

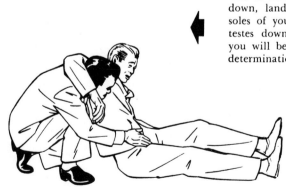